BUILDING BETTER GRAMMAR

BUILDING
BETTER
GRAMMAR

Gina Baaklini Hogan
Citrus Community College

WADSWORTH
CENGAGE Learning·

Australia • Brazil • Japan • Korea • Mexico • Singapore • Spain • United Kingdom • United States

WADSWORTH
CENGAGE Learning·

Building Better Grammar
Gina Baaklini Hogan

Senior Publisher: Lyn Uhl

Director of Developmental Studies: Annie Todd

Development Editor: Marita Sermolins

Assistant Editor: Elizabeth Rice

Editorial Assistant: Matthew Conte

Media Editor: Amy Gibbons

Marketing Coordinator: Brittany Blais

Marketing Communications Manager: Linda Yip

Art Director: Cate Barr

Print Buyer: Betsy Donaghey

Production Service: S4Carlisle Publishing Services

Compositor: S4Carlisle Publishing Services

For product information and technology assistance, contact us at **Cengage Learning Customer & Sales Support, 1-800-354-9706**

For permission to use material from this text or product, submit all requests online at **cengage.com/permissions** Further permissions questions can be emailed to **permissionrequest@cengage.com**

Library of Congress Control Number: 2011944306

ISBN-13: 978-0-495-90514-1

ISBN-10: 0-495-90514-3

Wadsworth
20 Channel Center
Street Boston, MA
02210 USA

Cengage Learning is a leading provider of customized learning solutions with office locations around the globe, including Singapore, the United Kingdom, Australia, Mexico, Brazil, and Japan. Locate your local office at: **international .cengage.com/region**

Cengage Learning products are represented in Canada by Nelson Education, Ltd.

For your course and learning solutions, visit **academic.cengage.com**

Purchase any of our products at your local college store or at our preferred online store **www.ichapters.com**

Printed in the United States of America
1 2 3 4 5 6 7 15 14 13 12 11

Table of Contents

UNIT THREE: Clauses and Kinds of Sentences

CHAPTER FIVE: The Fifth Building Block
Clauses   110

CHAPTER SIX: The Sixth Building Block
Kinds of Sentences   120

CHAPTER SEVEN: The Seventh Building Block
Avoiding Common Sentence Errors   150

Preface

BUILDING BLOCKS OF WRITING

Sentence construction is an essential skill for college writing. It helps create concise and clear paragraphs, essays, research papers, or reports. Teaching grammar in blocks as part of a building activity provides students with an easy-to-remember image that helps them understand and apply good sentence construction. This building process helps students to see how each grammar concept or building block sets the foundation for the next concept or building block; as a result, their confidence in writing grows the more they learn and practice. In my classes, I teach that the first foundational block is writing correct sentences, the second is writing effective paragraphs, and finally, writing effective essays. Just as real concrete foundations require specific raw materials (sand, water, cement, and gravel) that bind and mold together into a design, each writing building block (grammar, paragraphs, and essays) requires specific ingredients. For example, in grammar, to build a correct sentence you need nouns, verbs, prepositions, conjunctions, and so on.

As the first book of the *Building Better* series, *Building Better Grammar* builds students' knowledge of effective sentence construction to get them to the next step of putting sentences together successfully for coherent paragraphs, covered in *Building Better Paragraphs,* as well as preparing students' foundational skills for essay writing, covered in *Building Better Essays.*

The *Building Better* series developed out of a need to help more students succeed in learning to write effectively. Teaching writing as a building activity where concepts build on each other has worked well in my developmental writing courses. This technique of "building writing" makes the writing process a manageable one because it allows students to practice each concept or block separately, to see how it shapes subsequent blocks, and to increase their understanding and confidence along the way. In addition, this series also developed out of necessity—a need for cost-effective books that offer simple, accurate, student-friendly explanations. Many writing books present grammar content in too complex a manner without enough opportunities for practice, or present so many topics that can simply overwhelm the student. The *Building Better* series evolved with developmental students in mind; however, the textbooks are designed to be flexible enough that all college students or writing instructors can use them as quick reference guides. Any student who needs help writing concise and grammatically correct sentences can benefit from the pedagogy of *Building Better Grammar.* Instructors looking for a rich focus on sentence construction, easy-to-remember, simple, and brief explanations, and a variety of practice exercises will find it in *Building Better Grammar*.

> "*Building Better Grammar* is simple, accessible, and clear. It's a great place to begin—more than a reference—and not just a workbook."
>
> —Elizabeth Sarcone, Delta State University

> "I see a trend after 18 years of college teaching. High school graduates know very little about grammar as they exit H.S., and I find I have to teach what has been left untaught. This text provides explanations of grammar that I really don't have time to teach during my lectures. I would use *Building Better Grammar* as assigned reading on my syllabus. It's that good. I trust the explanation given herein."
>
> —Barbara Davis, Yavapai College

HALLMARKS OF *BUILDING BETTER GRAMMAR*

The Building Block Organization

Why organize grammar instruction into this unique building block manner? Students struggle to figure out how to construct grammatically sound sentences. Yet, once Gina Hogan played with when and how she presented the grammar concepts in her classes, she found that students who learn the basic elements of a sentence (like subjects, verbs, and prepositions) first gain great confidence and proficiency in the elements a complete sentence should have. Then, when they transition to building more challenging sentences (like compound, complex, and compound-complex), they retain their proficiency in keeping intact the basic structure of a complete sentence, yet they feel comfortable in adjusting the format to achieve more variety, and their confidence in their writing capabilities increases.

By providing students with the elements needed for effective sentences—subjects, verbs, conjunctions, prepositions, and much more—students will feel encouraged to write their own sentences. Realistic model sentences demonstrate the kind of sentence writing expected of students.

> "Many times textbooks heavily emphasize terminology instead of practicality.... The approach proposed for *Building Better Grammar* seems to be more in line with streamlining some of the wordiness involved that may sometimes turn off students and some instructors alike. Breaking down the learning process so that it builds upon itself makes good sense. Developmental English learners cannot be assumed to know or understand some precepts, and this approach of covering material before we build upon it might work wonders for comprehension and application."
>
> —Maria Villar-Smith, Miami Dade College

Building Skills

Students being introduced to writing sentences need a clear, consistent approach to feel comfortable with a task they feel is insurmountable. Developing writers are also usually developing readers, so Gina Hogan has been careful to simply explain all the concepts related to building or writing grammatically sound sentences. The chapters flow into gently encouraging students to apply their building sentence skills to editing fiction and nonfiction texts and to writing on different topics in preparation for academic writing.

Students participate in real, structured writing exercises throughout the chapters of *Building Better Grammar*. The Building Skills exercises ask students to employ increased levels of effort and independence with varied opportunities to immediately practice newly learned skills, transitioning from identifying successful sentence writing in practice sets to producing their own effective sentences. Engaging, modern subjects in the Building Skills exercises serve to stimulate and encourage inventive writing from your students. These exercises increase successively in difficulty and provide students with practice in editing, so they can improve in spotting grammar errors in their own writing. Building Skills Together exercises promotes collaborative work essential to writing and engagement among students. The Chapter Skills Review at the end of each chapter provides comprehensive practice for each grammar concept and can be used as a post-test or a chapter or diagnostic quiz.

"I'm very impressed with the clarity presented here, and I truly appreciate the practice sets! I so enjoy looking over the exercises here and imagining how I would employ individual and group work while covering this material. Students will gain excellent practice with each set of exercises designed for the new concepts presented. This allows for practice before the instruction is forgotten. Students get to employ what they are learning immediately! The exercises are fun and challenging. I sense confidence will be gained upon the completion of the exercises both in class and at home."
—Traci Gourdine, American River College

"At first I was surprised that you had students write a paragraph right in the middle of the text because composition skills would be worked on much later. But the method you used—having students answer questions about college stress using correct verb tenses and then put those answers into an organized paragraph—was a great idea, one which I will definitely use in the future. A seamless move from grammar to composition."
—Michael Duffy, Moorpark College

Memory Tips

Memory Tips present students with inventive, class-tested methods for remembering writing conventions and processes, many times with a unique mnemonic device. By highlighting important concepts, students can remember the steps to sentence construction and feel empowered when they set out to do the task on their own.

> "I like that prior concepts are repeated with a variation in wording and approach, such as the first Memory Tip box in Chapter 6. This encourages students to learn the concept, not just memorize rules without understanding."
> —Linda Eicken, Cape Fear Community College

ADDITIONAL RESOURCES

Instructor's Resource Manual. By Gina Hogan of Citrus Community College. Streamline and maximize the effectiveness of your course preparation using such resources as complete answer keys to Building Skills and Building Skills Together exercises, as well as Teaching Tips designed to guide instructors through teaching each chapter.

Instructor Companion Site. The *Building Better* series Instructor Companion Website includes password-protected PowerPoint slides to accompany the text, additional quizzing, and a digital version of the Instructor's Resource Manual. Instructors can register for access to this resource at login.cengage.com.

Aplia for Basic Writing Levels 1 and 2. Founded in 2000 by economist and Stanford professor Paul Romer, Aplia is dedicated to improving learning by increasing student effort and engagement. Aplia is an online, auto-graded homework solution that keeps your students engaged and prepared for class and has been used by more than 850,000 students at over 850 institutions. Aplia's online solutions provide developmental writing students with clear, succinct, and engaging writing instruction and practice to help them build the confidence they need to master basic writing and grammar skills. Aplia for Basic Writing: Level 1 (Sentence to Paragraph) and Aplia for Basic Writing: Level 2 (Paragraph to Essay) feature ongoing individualized practice, immediate feedback, and grades that can be automatically uploaded, so instructors can see where students are having difficulty (allowing for personalized assistance). Visit www.aplia.com/cengage for more details.

ACKNOWLEDGEMENTS

I am grateful to my parents, who instilled in me a strong love for learning and teaching. I deeply appreciate my husband and children for their enduring support and constant encouragement. I extend my ongoing gratitude to all college students, but especially developmental students, who allow me to be part of their academic journeys.

I am indebted more than I can say to Annie Todd at Cengage Learning for her belief in the *Building Better* series and their author. I extend a huge thanks to Marita Sermolins, my Development Editor, for her expertise, dedication, and thoughtful supervision. I offer my heartfelt gratitude to Judith Kunst for her excellent reviewing, accuracy checking, and editing.

Much gratitude and appreciation is due the many colleagues around the country whose helpful feedback informed many parts of this book:

Karen Abele, Sauk Valley Community College

Cheyenne Adams, Del Mar College

Matthew Allen, Wright College

Rachel Beckner, Western Oklahoma State College

Thomas Beery, Rhodes State College

Steven Berman, Oakland Community College

Jolan Bishop, Southeastern Community College

Randy Boone, Northampton Community College

Peggy Brent, Hinds Community College

Bessie Brown, Hinds Community College

Steven Budd, Los Medanos College

Judy Covington, Trident Technical College

James Crooks, Shasta College

Barbara Davis, Yavapai College

Nicole DeKasha, Elgin Community College

Margie Dernaika, Southwest Tennessee Community College

Joann Donigan, Delaware Valley College

Michael Duffy, Moorpark College

Linda Eicken, Cape Fear Community College

Traci Gourdine, American River College

Judith Harper, SUNY Adirondack

Elaine Herrick, Temple College

Leslie Hope, Los Angeles Valley College

Terry Irish, Clackamas Community College

Kimberlie Johnson, North Idaho College

Jill Lahnstein, Cape Fear Community College

Anna Maheshwari, Schoolcraft College

Kristene McClure, Glendale Community College
Lori Morrow, Rose State College
Susan Plachta, St. Clair County Community College
Stephanie Richardson, Genesee Community College
Marsha Rutter, Southwestern College
Elizabeth Sarcone, Delta State University
James Sodon, St. Louis Community College—Florissant Valley
Lynn Steiner, Cuesta College
Robert Stuber, Minnesota State Colleges—Southeast Technical
Suba Subbarao, Oakland Community College
Sheri Van Court, Brookhaven College
Maria Villar-Smith, Miami Dade College
Lynn Watson, Santa Rosa Junior College

Finally, my acknowledgement section is not complete without this: I dedicate this book to my wonderful family—Halim, Hiam, Bill, Remy, and Christopher. Your steadfast belief in me gives me wings to fly high!

UNIT ONE: Subjects, Verbs, and Subject-Verb Agreement

CHAPTER ONE: The First Building Block
Subjects

If you tell a friend that you just saw a movie you really enjoyed, your friend is likely to ask, "What is it about?" When we study grammar, that same question is among the first things we ask when presented with a single sentence. What is it about? "Subject" is grammar's name for the answer to that question, and learning to identify the subject in any sentence is the first building block to good writing.

The words you use to describe what the movie is about to your friend will probably start like this:

"A boy who . . ."

"Monsters that . . ."

"A town that . . ."

"It is . . ."

Of course, you will also tell your friend what the *boy,* the *monsters,* the *town,* or *it* did, but these words establish who or what you are discussing. Words that tell who or what *is doing* or *being something* are **subjects**. In grammar, subjects in sentences are words that come in the forms of **nouns** and **pronouns**.

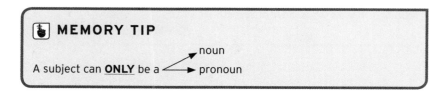

Nouns and pronouns help indicate the "doer" or "actor" in each sentence, and they are two **parts of speech**.

MEMORY TIP

Traditional grammar classifies words into eight basic types called **parts of speech**. It is important to recognize and identify the eight different parts of speech, so that you can understand grammar explanations and use the right word form in the right place.

- nouns
- pronouns
- verbs
- prepositions

- conjunctions
- adjectives
- adverbs
- interjections

See Appendix A on page 239 for a complete explanation.

NOUNS

A **noun** is a word that names a person, place, thing, idea, or activity. Nouns may function as subjects in sentences. Nouns are used to label things, places, and people, creating a common language between human beings. If people did not use nouns, they would be pointing and gesturing to one another rather than speaking actual words. A noun can name a:

- **Person:** "stranger" is the name given to a person with whom we come into contact in some way, but whom we do not know.
- **Place:** "mountain" is the name given to a high and often rocky area of a land mass with steep or sloping sides.
- **Thing:** "radar" is the name given to electronic equipment that transmits and receives high-frequency radio waves to detect or track distant objects.
- **Idea:** "democracy" is the name given to a way of organizing human society which allows and encourages all people in a given community or country to choose their leaders through a voting process.
- **Activity:** "studying" is the name given to the process of learning about a subject through careful reading and thinking. Nouns that name activities may be gerunds or nouns formed from verbs.

 MEMORY TIP

Some nouns are formed from verbs. These nouns are called **gerunds** and are formed by adding *-ing* to a verb to name an activity; for example, *talking, swimming, sewing,* or *cooking.* Gerunds can be subjects in a sentence.

Cooking is fun.

Singular and Plural Nouns

Nouns come in singular or plural forms.

- **Singular nouns** refer to <u>one</u> person, place, idea, activity, or thing.

      boy   town   box

- **Plural nouns** refer to <u>two or more</u> people, places, ideas, activities, or things. To form the plural noun, add *–s* or *–es* to the singular noun; a few nouns change spelling in other ways to form the plural; and a few stay the same regardless of number.

Add *–s* or *–es*:	boy/boys	town/towns	box/boxes
Change the spelling:	child/children	man/men	medium/media
Same spelling:	sheep/sheep	fish/fish	

Types of Nouns

Labels for all the people, places, and things we have encountered over hundreds of years now number into the tens of thousands, and new nouns are being added all the time. It is helpful to divide such a big group into smaller categories, so four different types of nouns exist:

1. **Proper Nouns**. A proper noun is a specific name of a place , a person, or a thing. The first letter of a proper noun is always capitalized no matter where it occurs in a sentence.

       Mr. Smith   Professor Hogan   California
       Los Angeles   Honda

2. **Common Nouns**. Common nouns are not capitalized and are ordinary and universal names that are assigned to things, people, or places.

       computer   tree   dog   chair   desk
       teacher   school   park   girl   boy

 MEMORY TIP

Remember a common noun is the general name to things, people, or places, whereas a proper noun is the specific and capitalized name to things, people, or places.

Common Noun	Proper Noun
cookie	Oreo
gelatin	Jello
facial tissue	Kleenex
restaurant	McDonald's
company	Ford Motor Company
film	Titanic

3. **Abstract Nouns**. Abstract nouns are names used for things that cannot be tasted, seen, touched, heard, or smelled, but are felt as an emotion or believed in as a philosophy.

freedom   love   trust   faith

4. **Collective Nouns**. Typically, words that identify more than one person, place, or thing are made plural in the English language, but collective nouns are an exception. Collective nouns name **groups** of people, things, or ideas as single entities. Words like *crew*, *team*, or *family* are single entities that are composed of at least two people. It takes at least two people to make a team, but the word *team* refers to one single entity or cluster of people.

> **group** (it takes more than one person to make up a group)
>
> **army** (it takes many soldiers to make an army)
>
> **jury** (it takes at least 12 members to make one jury)

Here are some more examples of collective nouns you might encounter.

council	minority	navy	department
public	school	senate	society
team	troupe	faculty	family
firm	group	jury	majority
army	audience	board	cabinet
class	committee	company	corporation

BUILDING SKILLS 1-1: Identifying Nouns

Identify the words below as one of the following nouns: proper, common, abstract, or collective.

Example: love   __abstract__

1. army _____

2. Mary Smith _____

3. committee _____

4. whale _____

5. truth _____

6. Peter _____

7. beauty _____

8. satellite _____

9. pavement _____

10. loyalty _____

BUILDING SKILLS 1-2: Identifying Nouns

Underline all the nouns in the following sentences.
Example: <u>Marissa</u> is a strong <u>swimmer</u>.

1. We had chicken at the Chinese restaurant; then, we had ice cream.
2. Love is not an easy emotion to understand.
3. Charlie and Mandy have had a good marital relationship for the last twenty years.
4. At the championship game, the excited spectators cheered loudly for the basketball team.
5. Yesterday, my brother and his friend sold tickets for the concert.
6. Anger leads to bad reactions such as physical or verbal abuse.
7. Mr. Redd is my favorite math teacher because he cares about his students.
8. McDonald's is where I have lunch every day because it is close to my office.
9. The Chicago Symphony plays a Mozart concerto once a year, so I never miss it.
10. The jury submitted its surprising verdict for the murder case.

BUILDING SKILLS 1-3: Identifying Common and Proper Nouns

Underline the common nouns <u>once</u> and the proper nouns <u>twice</u>.

The weather was warm and sunny, so Mary and Ginny decided to go on a picnic at Huntington Beach. In their red picnic hamper, they placed four ham sandwiches, two Granny Smith apples, a jug of lemonade, and six chocolate cookies. They packed their foldout chairs and beach ball. Before they left the house, they applied sunscreen lotion on their arms and legs and grabbed their straw hats. Although the beach was crowded with beachgoers, Mary and Ginny found a good picnic location away from the crowded Dan's Surf Shop and Starbucks café.

BUILDING SKILLS 1-4: Working with Nouns

In small groups, write a short paragraph about a public place such as a park, restaurant, or library. Use the following prompts to describe the public place.

1. Three different sentences using a proper noun in each sentence.

_____

_____

_____

_____

_____

2. Three different sentences using a common noun in each sentence.

_____

_____

_____

_____

_____

3. Two different sentences using collective nouns in each sentence.

_____

_____

_____

_____

_____

4. One sentence using an abstract noun.

_____

_____

_____

_____

_____

❙ BUILDING SKILLS TOGETHER 1-1: Writing with Nouns

In small groups, write a paragraph of five to ten sentences using various nouns to describe an ideal vacation. Once you have completed your sentences, underline all the nouns in your paragraph.

_____

_____

_____

_____

_____

_____

_____

_____

_____

_____

_____

_____

_____

_____

PRONOUNS

Subjects in sentences may be nouns or pronouns. Whereas a noun labels a person, thing, place, or activity, a **pronoun** names a person or thing doing or being something in a sentence. Pronouns come in many forms, and Chapter Four will provide detailed explanations. However, two main types of pronouns—**subject pronouns** and **indefinite pronouns**—are essential to your understanding of actors or subjects in sentences.

Subject Pronouns

A pronoun that identifies and names the specific person or thing doing or being something in a sentence is a **subject pronoun.** The subject pronouns—*I, you, he, she, it, we,* and *they*—function as the person or thing doing or being something in the sentence.

I ate the last piece of pizza.
> *I* identifies the person who is eating in this sentence.

You need to submit the completed application form to the supervisor.
> *You* identifies the person who needs to submit in this sentence.

He asked about the election votes.
> *He* identifies the person who is asking in this sentence.

It had big letters on the side and a blaring horn.
> *It* identifies the thing in this sentence.

We need to ensure the diving equipment is working properly.
> *We* identifies the person in this sentence.

<u>They</u> went mountain climbing during the worst weather.

They identifies the person in this sentence.

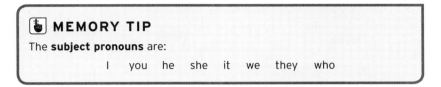

MEMORY TIP

The **subject pronouns** are:

I you he she it we they who

Subject pronouns also replace nouns to reduce repetition. Consider this paragraph:

<u>Mary</u> has trouble with time. <u>Mary</u> often goes to bed late, and <u>Mary</u> gets up late the next morning. <u>Mary</u> often misses her ride to work, and <u>Mary</u> gets in trouble with her boss. Recently, <u>Mary</u> did not schedule into her calendar her online college registration appointment. As a result, <u>Mary</u> missed registering for any classes for the fall semester. <u>Mary</u> has to try adding the classes instead.

In this paragraph, the noun *Mary* is stated so many times that it distracts the reader and makes the paragraph boring to read. To fix this problem, pronouns can be used in place of the nouns to clarify and enliven the paragraph.

Mary has trouble with time. <u>She</u> often goes to bed late, and <u>she</u> gets up late the next morning. <u>She</u> often misses her ride to work, and <u>she</u> gets in trouble with her boss. Recently, <u>she</u> did not schedule into her calendar her online college registration appointment. As a result, <u>she</u> missed registering for any classes for the fall semester. <u>She</u> has to try adding the classes instead.

Whether they stand alone or replace nouns in sentences, the pronouns *I, you, he, she, it, we,* and *they* may be used as the subject in sentences.

BUILDING SKILLS 1-5: Subject Pronouns

Underline the subject pronouns in the following sentences. Some sentences may have more than one subject pronoun.

Example: <u>I</u> want to participate in the running marathon this year.

1. She is my best friend, and she helps me with everything.

2. They ran down to the lake for a swim because it was too hot.

3. It rained all day yesterday, and I felt miserable.

4. We worked hard and long on our physics project.

5. He gives good advice because he is a wonderful counselor.

6. Cooking is hard for me, so I avoid it.

7. For hours we waited outside in the rain for a glimpse of the celebrity.

8. When the cat pounced on the mouse, it shrieked.

9. Chemistry is a difficult subject, but I work hard at understanding it.

10. They played a dirty trick on the poor, helpless child.

BUILDING SKILLS 1-6: Nouns and Pronouns

Underline the noun(s) in each sentence, and, on the provided line, replace with the appropriate subject pronoun.

Example: Every morning, <u>Billy Lee and Clarissa</u> go for a walk. <u> they </u>

1. James and Sara will get married next June. _____

2. The girl brought a chocolate cake for the gathering. _____

3. The musician finished his solo performance. _____

4. Anxious, Jerry called his ill girlfriend. _____

5. During the storm, the big oak tree fell on my mother's car. _____

Indefinite Pronouns

Another type of pronoun that can function as the subject in a sentence is the indefinite pronoun. An **indefinite pronoun** does not refer to any specific person or thing, so it is vague and "not definite." Even though they refer to a less clearly identified noun, indefinite pronouns often take the function of the subject in the sentence. These are the most common indefinite pronouns:

anybody	nobody	somebody	everybody
anything	nothing	something	everything
anyone	no one	someone	everyone
each	either	neither	none

<u>Anyone</u> can contribute to the project.

<u>Most</u> were asleep when the fire alarm went off.

<u>None</u> of the food is fresh.

BUILDING SKILLS 1-7: Indefinite Pronouns

Replace the underlined words in each sentence with an indefinite pronoun from the box of words provided.

anybody	nobody	somebody	everybody
anything	nothing	something	everything
anyone	no one	someone	everyone
each	either	neither	none

Example: <u>Every single thing</u> in life has a price.   <u> Everything </u>

1. Does <u>any student</u> have a question?   _____

2. Give this to <u>any person</u> in the class.   _____

3. <u>Not one person</u> knew how to solve the math problem.   _____

4. Is there <u>some person</u> who knows how to use this machine? _____

5. <u>Every single person</u> danced to the music.   _____

6. There must be <u>a person</u> who can play the piano.   _____

7. <u>Some single thing</u> should be done about his behavior.   _____

8. <u>Every single one</u> of the voters voted yes.   _____

9. <u>Not a single person</u> could stay after school.   _____

10. <u>One of the people</u> in the club fainted.   _____

IDENTIFYING THE SUBJECT

Your understanding of nouns and pronouns will help you recognize subjects in sentences. Learning to identify the subject in any sentence is the first building block to good writing. A **sentence** is a group of words that expresses a complete thought.

Arrived early.

What does this group of words tell you? Not much. You are left asking "*Who* or *what* arrived early?" The "who" or "what" is not identified here, so we do not know the subject in this sentence. Each sentence must have a subject that tells who or what is doing something or who or what is being described.

Gina arrived early.

Who or what arrived early? Gina. This is then the subject or the "who" that arrived early. Just as the words *Arrived early* cannot stand alone without an actor (Gina), so the word *Gina* cannot stand alone without an action. A correct sentence must express a complete thought or have a full meaning that stands by itself. That completion or independence requires BOTH a **subject** (actor) and a **verb** (action). Verbs are the second building block of grammar and will be defined in the next chapter.

In any sentence, the subject tells the reader who or what is doing or being something. To locate the subject in a sentence, always ask *Who or what is doing or being something?*

> **Mary is my sister.**

Who or what *is* my sister? A person named Mary. Since you know subjects can ONLY be nouns or pronouns, check your answer: Is Mary a noun or pronoun? It is a proper noun; thus, it is the subject in the sentence. Of course, this sentence may have included a pronoun as a subject like so:

> <u>She</u> **is my sister.**

> <u>He</u> **listens to his iPod.**

To determine the subject in this sentence, ask *who or what is doing the listening?* The answer is he. Is the word *he* a noun or pronoun? It is a pronoun. You know that the subject can only be a noun or pronoun; therefore, *he* must be the subject in the sentence, and it is the pronoun doing the action. Of course, this sentence may have included a noun as subject.

> <u>John</u> **listens to his iPod.**

 MEMORY TIP

To find the **subject** of a sentence, ask yourself : *"who or what is doing or being something?"*

The answer to that question must always be a **noun** or a **pronoun**.

SIMPLE AND COMPOUND SUBJECTS

A complete sentence has the subject as one of its main building blocks. The number of subjects in a sentence determines whether the sentence has a simple or compound subject.

1. **Simple subject.** When a sentence has one noun or pronoun doing the action, that sentence has one subject known as a simple subject.

   > **Daniel plays the drums.**
   > Who plays the drums?
   > Daniel ← one noun

   Because there is one subject, the sentence has a **simple subject**.

2. **Compound subject.** The word *compound* means a combination of at least two things. When a sentence has two or more nouns or pronouns doing the same action, those are called compound subjects.

Daniel and Marty play the drums.

Who plays the drums?

Daniel and Marty ← two nouns.

Because there are two subjects, the sentence has a **compound subject**.

👆 **MEMORY TIP**

1 subject   = simple subject
2 or more subjects = compound subjects

Note: The word **and** between words often signifies that there may be compound elements.

BUILDING SKILLS 1-8: Simple and Compound Subjects

Underline the subject in each sentence and determine if the subject is simple (SS) or compound (CS). Remember: Subjects can be nouns or pronouns.

Example: SS The factory has a good reputation among the residents of this neighborhood.

_____ 1. Frank and Ginnie danced all night at the Vanity Fair Ball.

_____ 2. Terry laughs hysterically at any joke.

_____ 3. I was surprised I did well on my biology exam even though I had not studied.

_____ 4. Letty and Tom had a hurtful argument.

_____ 5. Someone stole the precious family heirloom from my grandmother's home.

_____ 6. *Coldplay* and *Maroon 5* are strong bands on the musical charts.

_____ 7. The new smartphone is not working well for me.

_____ 8. Math and English are my worst subjects.

_____ 9. The container truck and the motorcycle crashed into each other.

_____ 10. Everyone came to the formal dance to see who will be named Dance Queen.

_____ 11. Jenny, Marissa, and Valerie are on the college's volleyball team.

_____ 12. Sports shows, talk shows, and late-night shows are my favorite television shows.

_____ 13. No one is telling the truth about this mysterious crime.

_____ 14. Tom and Terry need a new computer for their office work.

_____ 15. We did not want to go to sleep after we saw that horror movie.

_____ 16. Nothing makes sense about this math problem.

_____ 17. She likes Chinese food more than Mexican food.

_____ 18. Lasagna and pizza are my family's favorite meals.

_____ 19. Somebody help this hurt child!

_____ 20. My cousin wants to become an emergency room nurse.

BUILDING SKILLS TOGETHER 1-2: Writing Simple and Compound Subjects

In small groups, compose eight sentences about a popular television show. Write four sentences with simple subjects and four sentences with compound subjects.

_____

_____

_____

_____

_____

_____

_____

_____

_____

_____

_____

_____

_____

_____

_____

_____

RECOGNIZING SUBJECTS IN TRICKY SITUATIONS

The first building block in a complete sentence is the subject. Learning to identify the subject correctly will allow you to add, subtract, switch, and evaluate additional elements to your sentences, bringing power and flexibility to your writing. Most often, the subject can easily be identified; however, at times it may be difficult to spot because of the structure of the sentence. Five specific sentence structures make identifying the subject tricky:

- Imperative sentences
- Sentences with prepositional phrases
- Declarative sentences with *here* and *there*
- Interrogative sentences
- Sentences with gerunds and infinitives

Subjects in Imperative Sentences

A subject may be invisible but understood in an **imperative sentence,** the name given to a sentence that issues a command.

Sit in that chair!

Who or what sits in that chair? This is an order or command, so the subject is whoever is receiving the command—you. In other words, the complete sentence is *You* sit in that chair! Because the subject of an imperative sentence is invisible yet understood, we call that subject the **"implied you."** Note that imperative or command sentences frequently end with an exclamation point to show strong emotion.

Please do not throw snowballs!

Who or what throws (or wants to throw) snowballs? *You* please avoid throwing snowballs.

BUILDING SKILLS 1-9: Identifying Implied Subjects

Read the sentences and write *yes* by the ones that have an implied subject and *no* by the ones that do not have an implied subject.

Example: <u>yes</u> Be careful as you cross the street.

_____ 1. Finish your homework!

_____ 2. My iPod is in its charging dock.

_____ 3. Call 911!

_____ 4. Take your time reading the history test.

_____ 5. His old car broke down on the way to work.

_____ 6. Stop annoying your sister!

_____ 7. John is cleaning his dirty room.

_____ 8. Shut off the cell phone!

_____ 9. They stopped by for a late dinner.

_____ 10. Please be home on time.

Subjects as Distinct from Prepositional Phrases

Preposition is the name given to words that signal place (*above, inside, behind*), time (*before, after, within*), or source (*to, from, for, of, by*). The word *preposition* comes from two Latin words that mean "placed before." Prepositions are words that can be placed before a noun or pronoun to show the relationship that exists between that noun or pronoun and some other word in the sentence. In fact, the prepositions *of, to,* and *in* are among the most frequently used words in English.

I wrote a letter <u>to</u> him.

The word *to* is a preposition. It shows the relationship between *letter* and *him*. There are many, many prepositions; some of the most common are listed here:

Place		Time	Source	
above	across	after	about	against
among	around	before	at	by
below	behind	during	because of	due to
beneath	beside	until	except	for
between	beyond	since	from	of
by	in/into		off	to
inside	near		toward	with
out	outside		without	here
over	on			
through	under			
up	upon			
within				

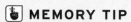 **MEMORY TIP**

An easy way to help you remember prepositions is to think of the expression *the house*. Then put as many prepositional words as you can in front of the words *the house*:

above the house	**from** the house
around the house	**with** the house
by the house	**to** the house
behind the house	**near** the house
between the house	**under** the house
of the house	**over** the house
off the house	**on** the house

Not all prepositions are one word long. Sometimes they may combine several words such as *next to, according to, because of, on account of, along with, in addition to,* and many more.

At other times, this part of speech commonly appears as part of a descriptive group of words called a **prepositional phrase**. An easy way to spot prepositional phrases is to recognize that such phrases begin with a preposition and end with a noun or pronoun.

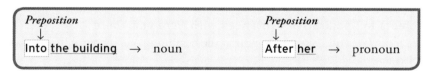

Prepositions and prepositional phrases provide additional information to the reader because they express the time, place, or source of the action, but they <u>do not</u> and <u>cannot</u> include the subject of the sentence. Help yourself locate the subject by crossing out the prepositional phrase to eliminate it from the sentence. Then look for the noun or pronoun.

Into the room walked Mother.

Step 1:   ~~Into the room~~ walked Mother.
Step 2:   Who or what walked? Mother
Step 3:   Mother is a noun and the subject in the sentence.

BUILDING SKILLS 1-10: Subjects with Prepositional Phrases

Cross out the prepositional phrases in the following sentences. Then, underline the subject(s).

Example: ~~Beneath the big oak tree~~ sat the <u>newlyweds</u>.

1. Under the porch and into a dirt hole slithered a long black snake.
2. In the darkness, the hungry wolf howled at the top of the mountain.
3. In the city downtown, a window washer dangled on the side of the tall building.
4. An abandoned cabin stood at the bottom of the valley.
5. The medical helicopter flew into the foggy night sky.
6. On a warm day, the little children played contentedly down by the stream.
7. Across the way and beyond the mysterious woods stands the majestic castle.
8. The marathon runners jogged victoriously toward the finish line.
9. To burn more calories, she jogged up the steep hill.
10. Under the dead body lay the bloody murder weapon.

Subjects in Declarative Sentences with *Here* and *There*

The words *here* and *there* may appear at the beginning of a sentence that declares a statement.

> Here is my book.

In such **declarative sentence**s, remember that *here* or *there* cannot function as the subject of a sentence because these two words are not nouns or pronouns. In fact, they are prepositions that show location, and prepositions cannot be the subject in the sentence. In trying to determine the subject in a sentence that begins with *here* and *there*, cross out the words *here* or *there* and flip the sentence around, so the noun or pronoun starts the sentence first.

> Here is my book.
>
> Change it to: My book is here.

Who or what is here? *My book.* The word *book* is a noun; therefore, it is the subject in the sentence.

BUILDING SKILLS 1-11: Subjects in Declarative Sentences with Here and There

Underline the subject(s) in each sentence.
Example: Here is my lost <u>passport</u>!

1. There was a party after the football game.
2. My Aunt Nessa and Uncle Vern are here for the reading of the will.
3. More dog food is there in that bag that is inside the pantry.
4. Here are the recipes and ingredients you need for the bake sale.
5. There is no news about the train accident to share with you.
6. Here is the announcement you wanted typed this morning.
7. There are many reasons for her deception.
8. Here comes Lynn's boyfriend with another girl.
9. The answer to that complicated question is right here.
10. Here is the major issue: she betrayed her friend.

Subjects in Interrogative Sentences

Interrogative sentences are sentences that ask questions and end with a question mark, such as: Where is my book? To spot the subject in these sentences, answer the question with a full statement, then try to identify the subject.

Where is my laptop?

You might answer: My laptop is on the table. Who or what is on the table? The laptop, which is a noun; therefore, it is the subject in the sentence.

BUILDING SKILLS 1-12: Subjects in Interrogative Sentences

Underline the subject in each sentence.
Example: Where is my brown leather <u>wallet?</u>

1. Where is the championship trophy for the quarterback?
2. Why is Sandy angry at Mindy?
3. Did Sara feed the two small children?
4. Did the male suspect confess to the gruesome murder?
5. What did the urgent e-mail she sent you say?

Turn each statement into a question then a command:

6. Harry is painting the garage.
   Question: _____
   Command: _____

7. Nancy helps with the project.
   Question: _____
   Command: _____

8. Doug left his backpack behind.
   Question: _____
   Command: _____

9. Mirabelle goes to her room.
   Question: _____
   Command: _____

10. The students turned in their tests.
    Question: _____
    Command: _____

Sentences with Gerunds and Infinitives as Subjects

Gerunds are verbs that function as nouns and have an *-ing* ending. Because gerunds are derived from verbs and have an *-ing* ending, they express action. However, gerunds may occupy slots traditionally held by nouns in sentences such as subjects. They do so when they name an activity such as *smoking, cooking, shopping,* or *exercising.* Gerunds may occur as one word, or they may be part of a gerund phrase.

Reading is my most relaxing summer activity.

Who or what is most relaxing? *Reading.* It is an activity; therefore, it is the gerund that is the subject in the sentence.

Eating on the run is one of the unhealthiest American habits.

Who or what is one of the unhealthiest American habits? *Eating on the run,* which is an activity or a gerund phrase that is the subject in the sentence.

Infinitives

The **infinitive** verb is the simplest base form of the verb, and the form that appears as the headword in dictionaries. For example, the dictionary entry or infinitive for *gossip* looks like this:

Gos.sip /gos'sip/ *n* **1** conversation about the personal details of other people's lives, whether rumor or fact, especially when malicious **2** someone who
habitually discusses the personal details of others' lives *vi* spread rumors

Because infinitives are derived from verbs, they do express actions or states of
being; however, in some sentences, they may function as nouns or subjects.

   Gossip spreads quickly at my workplace.

This sentence is about the activity or the noun *gossip,* which is the subject in the
sentence.

   The *to* infinitive is the base form of the verb preceded by the word *to.* It forms
noun phrases, which can be subjects.

   To graduate from college is my greatest achievement.

Who or what is my greatest achievement? *To graduate,* which is an infinitive
functioning as the noun that is the subject in the sentence.

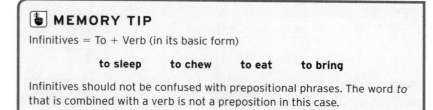

> ## 🖱 MEMORY TIP
>
> Infinitives = To + Verb (in its basic form)
>
> **to sleep   to chew   to eat   to bring**
>
> Infinitives should not be confused with prepositional phrases. The word *to*
> that is combined with a verb is not a preposition in this case.

BUILDING SKILLS 1-13: Subjects as Gerunds and Infinitives

Underline the subject in each sentence and write *gerund* or *infinitive* on
each line.

Example: <u>gerund</u> <u>Talking</u> loudly is not allowed in the chapel.

_____ 1. To learn about crimes is all I want to do.

_____ 2. Playing basketball requires physical strength.

_____ 3. To sleep is the only thing Jenny wants to do after her double
shift at the diner.

_____ 4. Winning the final soccer game surprised our team.

_____ 5. To put out the campfire was John's responsibility.

_____ 6. Working nights can be difficult when one is a single parent.

_____ 7. Singing on national television is the dream of many people.

_____ 8. To read to pediatric cancer patients is Nora's noble contribution.

_____ 9. Drinking alcohol, like smoking, should be banned from restaurants.

_____ 10. To find a wedding dress is every bride's main task after deciding to marry.

▮ BUILDING SKILLS TOGETHER 1-3: Subjects in Sentences

Working with a partner or small group, complete the following tasks:

1. Write three imperative sentences.

_____

_____

_____

_____

_____

2. Write three sentences with prepositional phrases.

_____

_____

_____

_____

_____

3. Write three declarative sentences.

_____

_____

_____

_____

_____

4.   Write three interrogative sentences.

_____

_____

_____

_____

_____

5.   Write four sentences with gerunds and infinitives as subjects.

_____

_____

_____

_____

_____

▌ BUILDING SKILLS TOGETHER 1-4: Subjects in Writing

In small groups, underline the subject or subjects in each sentence.

(1) College students do not get good grades for their health habits. (2) Often on their own for the first time, college students leave behind their families' way of eating, sleeping, and relaxing and develop new habits and routines—usually not healthier ones. (3) Sometimes, students do not get enough sleep or keep irregular schedules that throw their sleep patterns off. (4) Often, there are not enough hours during the day for all the things students need or want to do such as study, socialize, pursue extracurricular activities, surf the Internet, work at part-time jobs, and participate in community service. (5) Sleeping less and juggling more causes students to become exhausted and suffer greater risks for colds, flu, digestive problems, and other maladies.

—Adapted from Dianne Hales, *An Invitation to Health*

▲ BUILDING SKILLS TOGETHER 1-5: Subjects in Writing

In small groups, underline the subject or subjects in each sentence. Then, determine the type of subject (noun or pronoun) and, when applicable, the tricky situation it is in (imperative, prepositional phrase, declarative with here and there, interrogative, gerund, or infinitive). The first sentence is done for you.

Noun
(1) The <u>bowl</u> was perfect. (2) It had real presence and sat on a coffee table. (3) Everyone, who has purchased a house or who has wanted to sell a house, was familiar with the tricks used to convince a buyer that the house is quite special: a cozy fire in the fireplace in the early evening; flowers in a pitcher on the kitchen counter; or the wafting aroma of spring from a single drop of scent vaporizer. (4) Andrea was a real-estate agent. (5) For prospective buyers who were dog lovers, she dropped off her dog at the same time she placed the bowl in the house that was up for sale. (6) She put a dish of water in the kitchen for Mondo, took his squeaking plastic frog out of her purse, and dropped it on the floor. (7) Tackling and whacking his favorite toy were Mondo's favorite activities. (8) The bowl, Andrea thought, was both subtle and noticeable. (9) Its glaze was the color of cream and seemed to glow no matter what light it was placed in. (10) There were a few bits of color in it—tiny geometric flashes. (11) Some of these bits were tinged with flecks of silver. (12) They were as mysterious as cells seen under a microscope. (13) It was difficult not to study them. (14) They shimmered, flashed for a split second, and then resumed their shape. (15) Something about the colors with their random placement suggested motion. (16) People who liked country furniture commented on the bowl. (17) It turned out that people who love antique furniture loved it just as much. (18) But the bowl was not all that ostentatious or even so noticeable. (19) No one suspected that it had been put in place deliberately. (20) Oftentimes, the owners, who were always asked to be away or to step outside when the house was being shown, did not even know that the bowl had been in their house. (21) Andrea was sure that the bowl brought her luck. (21) Bids were often put in on the houses that had the bowl. (22) What magic did this bowl hold?

—From Ann Beattie's Janus

CHAPTER ONE SKILLS REVIEW: Subjects

Underline or insert the subject(s) in the following sentences.

1. Leave your iPod here.

2. Staying with his mother is not an option.

3. Through the castle's halls echoed the sound of joyful music.

4. There was a crowd at the Virgin Records store because of the new hit album.

5. Under a pile of leaves slithered a poisonous black snake.

6. Stop trying to bother me!

7. There was a call for you from your girlfriend.

8. Anyone could have broken into the bank's safe.

9. Into the field rode the prized white horse.

10. Finish your chores before you go with your friends.

11. Do not decorate that vase in that way!

12. Somebody ate all the hidden candy.

13. To pay taxes is the obligation of every American citizen.

14. Across the street and on the corner stood a suspicious-looking man.

15. Around the house was the gruesome evidence of the murder.

16. After months of practice, Emily and Cameron won the running marathon.

17. Everyone is gathered for a celebration in the hall.

18. Owen, Pat, and Aaron all live together in one tiny apartment.

19. Here come John and Jim with the election banner.

20. Will Bob and Wade be at the department meeting at 2 P.M.?

21. Anything could happen in a desert storm.

22. Securing an agreement with the rebels was the president's primary goal.

23. There was a long line at the bookstore today.

24. Something is not right with this income statement.

25. Among the garden flowers sat a quiet child with a teddy bear.

CHAPTER TWO: The Second Building Block
Verbs

When your friend asks you what your favorite movie is about, you may say, "Zombies," but your friend will want more information than that. What do the zombies do? How did they become zombies? What happens to them in the end? A movie, after all, is a *moving* picture—the action is the whole point. A sentence, too, must have action. The action of a sentence can be huge, like an airplane crashing into a mountain, or tiny, like a pencil resting on a table. Big or small, the words that show the action of a sentence are called **verbs**. Verbs are the second building block in grammar. Complete sentences must have subjects and verbs.

ACTION AND BEING VERBS

Every complete sentence must have a verb. Any words that show what someone or something does, did, or will do, or what someone or something is, was, or will be are called **verbs**. To find verbs in a sentence, we need to find the subject in the sentence and ask the following question: What is the subject *doing* or *being*?

> He <u>kicks</u> the ball to the other players.
> He <u>is</u> a new member of the team.

The subject in both of these sentences is the pronoun *he*. The verbs are *kicks* (action) and *is* (being).

Verbs come in two main types: action or being verbs.

1. **Action verbs** or verbs that show what the subject does, did, or will do. Examples of action verbs include: *jump, eat, play, sleep, speak, walk, move, feed, practice,* and hundreds more.

   > She <u>moved</u> the table.
   > She <u>practiced</u> the piano.

BUILDING SKILLS 2-1: Action Verbs

Underline the action verb in each of the following sentences.

Example: Mark <u>crashed</u> his new car yesterday.

1. Sylvia <u>edits</u> her essay after she writes it.
2. Everyone <u>talks</u> about the amazing new movie.
3. Robin <u>sings</u> and dances beautifully.
4. Impatiently, we <u>wait</u> for the judge's decision.
5. They <u>announced</u> the contest winner on Friday.
6. Ron and Elaine both <u>got</u> big prizes.
7. At artwork, she <u>draws</u> slowly but carefully.
8. Gerald <u>practices</u> for the Olympic Games.
9. She <u>performs</u> some difficult dance steps.
10. They always <u>invite</u> us to their chili cook-off.

---

2. **Being verbs** are verbs that show what someone or something is, was, or will be. Examples of being verbs include the verb *to be*: *is, am, are, was, were, will be*.

   > This action movie <u>is</u> funny.
   > I <u>am</u> hungry.

 MEMORY TIP

The most problematic verb in the English language is the verb ***to be***. It is made up of the following words:

	Present	Past	Future
I	am	was	will be
You	are	were	will be
He/she/it	is	was	will be
We	are	were	will be
They	are	were	will be

BUILDING SKILLS 2-2: Being Verbs

Underline the being verbs in each of the following sentences.

Example: She <u>is</u> the sister of the newly elected governor.

1. The state fair <u>is</u> a big treat for children.
2. I <u>am</u> the wife of a powerful man.

3. We are all excellent pie bakers.

4. The judges are experts in these contests.

5. One farmer's house was the place where the tornado touched down.

6. The dress will be a gorgeous blue-green creation.

7. I will be a lawyer by the time I turn twenty-five.

8. They were a marvelous group of creative quilt-makers.

9. I am fond of mystery novels set in the Regency era.

10. He was a friendly clerk at the old bank.

🕯 BUILDING SKILLS TOGETHER 2-1: Action and Being Verbs

In small groups, read this paragraph and underline the action or being verb in each sentence.

(1) Experts in the field of archaeology study the life ways of people from the past by excavating and analyzing the material people left behind. (2) The purpose of archaeology is not to fill up museums by collecting exotic relics from prehistoric societies. (3) Rather, it is to understand cultural adaptations of ancient people by reconstructing their cultures. (4) Archaeologists concentrate on societies of the past, so they are limited to working with material remains such as written records. (5) From these material remains, archaeologists are able to infer many cultural aspects including ideas and behavior patterns held by people thousands or millions of years ago.

— From Ferrari/Andreatta, *Cultural Anthropology: An Applied Perspective*

SIMPLE AND COMPOUND VERBS

Like subjects, verbs can be counted in a sentence. If there is one verb in the sentence, it is a **simple verb**.

Jenny dances beautifully.

What can Jenny do? Dance. This sentence has one verb or a simple verb.
If there are two or more verbs in the sentence, they are **compound verbs**.

Jenny dances and sings beautifully.

What can Jenny do? Dance and sing. This sentence has two verbs or compound verbs.

> ### 🖐 MEMORY TIP
> The word *compound* means a combination of at least two things. The word *and* between words often indicates compound elements.

BUILDING SKILLS 2-3: Simple and Compound Verbs

Underline the verbs and identify the verbs as simple or compound on the lines.

Example: They <u>argued</u> and <u>fought</u> all night long.   <u>Compound</u>

1. The train screeched and rumbled loudly into the busy station. _____

2. My sister entered and won the contest for best artist. _____

3. The referee lost count of the tennis balls. _____

4. I prepared the vegetables and cooked the meat for tonight's dinner. _____

5. The plumber broke and removed the rusted water pipe. _____

6. The international flags fluttered in the wind. _____

7. He read the signs carefully and followed the winding road to his destination. _____

8. The sun came through the window and faded the expensive tablecloth. _____

9. They danced until the music stopped. _____

10. My unfriendly dog barks and growls at strangers. _____

VERB TENSES

Verbs are tools that can help you express time in your sentences. **Tense** is the form of the verb that shows at what time the subject is performing the action. **Past**, **present**, and **future** are the basic categories of time, and therefore represent the three major tenses.

Past	Present	Future
(All time before now)	(Now)	(All time beyond now)
Talked	Talk	Will talk

Within each of those three tenses, there are four additional forms that allow a writer to describe extremely specific times in which things happen.

	Simple	Perfect	Progressive	Perfect Progressive
Present	She writes	She has written	She is writing	She has been writing
Past	She wrote	She had written	She was writing	She had been writing
Future	She will write	She will have written	She will be writing	She will have been writing

Altogether, then, there are twelve tenses. To learn these tenses and get used to the various shifts you can make, you need to practice moving single verbs through all twelve tenses. That practice is called **conjugation**. In order to understand how to conjugate through the tenses, remember that the subject, whether it is a noun or a pronoun, determines the form of the verb. This group of **subject pronouns** provides a clear and simple way to move a verb through conjugation:

I	walk
You	walk
He/she/it	walks
We	walk
They	walk

Notice that the ending on the verb for *he/she/it* changes. That is the effect of the subject's number on the verb. Chapter Three, "Subject-Verb Agreement," explains this effect.

The Simple Tense

The **simple tense** shows that an action or state of being happens simply in four ways:

- now (in the present)
- yesterday (sometime in the past)
- tomorrow (sometime in the future)
- habitually (over and over again across time)

Simple Present

The **simple present** tense shows that an action or state of being is happening now. It is used to describe a <u>present situation</u>.

I eat a hearty breakfast in the morning.

It is also used for <u>regular routines or habits</u>. You can use words like *always, usually, never, every day*, and *twice a week* to show how often.

I go to work every day.

He often buys the newspaper from the corner vendor.

It may also be used to describe <u>general truths</u> as scientific facts.

Once every 28 days, the moon circles the earth.

 MEMORY TIP

With the present verb tense, the subject changes the ending of the verb. The change is most apparent when the subject is a third person (he or she or it). Then, the verb must have an -s added to the end.

He stud<u>ies</u> for his medical exams.

She cal<u>ls</u> the paramedics every time her father falls.

It set<u>s</u> in the West and rises in the East.

If the verb is not an action but a *to be* verb, keep in mind that the verb *to be* changes depending on the subject pronoun.

 MEMORY TIP

The most problematic verb in the English language is the verb *to be*. It is conjugated like this:

	Present	Past	Future
I	am	was	will be
You	are	were	will be
He/she/it	is	was	will be
We	are	were	will be
They	are	were	will be

BUILDING SKILLS 2-4: Simple Present Tense

Write a sentence using the simple present tense for each of the verbs given.
Example: <u>write</u>   I <u>write</u> in my diary every night.

1. stop

_____

2. catch

_____

3. speak

_____

4. hope

_____

5. watch

_____

_____

BUILDING SKILLS 2-5: Simple Present Tense

Underline the simple present verbs in each sentence and identify the purpose behind its use (present situation, habitual, or general facts).

Example: <u>habitual</u> They <u>go</u> to the movie theater every Saturday morning.

_____ 1. Every Wednesday, Mrs. Pauley drives her three children to dance practice.

_____ 2. Usually, I work as a lab assistant at JPL, but now, I am on leave of absence for two months.

_____ 3. The earth is 4.5 billion years old.

_____ 4. In the afternoons, I usually take a fifteen-minute nap before I start my paperwork.

_____ 5. It takes light 8 min. 20 sec. to travel from the sun to the earth.

_____

Simple Past

The **simple past** tense shows that an action happened at a point in the past and is over now. You can use words like _before, yesterday, years ago, in the past,_ and many more to indicate this tense in your writing. With most verbs, this verb tense is indicated with the addition of _–ed_ at the end of the verb.

Yesterday, I <u>talked</u> to John about the camping trip.

 MEMORY TIP

Verbs that take an _-ed_ ending to change to past tense are called **regular verbs**. Most verbs in English are regular.

BUILDING SKILLS 2-6: Simple Past Tense

In the following sentences, underline the verbs and write them in past tense on the provided lines.

Example: The nervous children <u>perform</u> during the long musical. <u>performed</u>

1. The car stops working on cold days. _____

2. The woman glares at me for buying the last book on the shelf. _____

3. They visit me in the summer for two weeks. _____

4. The invisible monster in the movie appears every two minutes. _____

5. My niece places her laptop on the gleaming wood floors. _____

Simple Future

The **simple future** tense shows that an action will happen in the future. To indicate this tense, you can use words like *tomorrow, next week or month, in the coming years,* and many more. To construct this verb tense, always add the word *will* before the verb.

I <u>will go</u> to the mall next week.

BUILDING SKILLS 2-7: Simple Future Tense

Complete the sentences with the simple future tense of the verb provided in parentheses.

Example: Next week, we (have) <u>will have</u> final exams.

1. Tomorrow, Mike (start) _____ his new job.

2. The seafood for the restaurant (come) _____ from Mr. Alexander's daily catch. I hope the downtown bus (be) _____ on time this once.

3. Lynn (earn) _____ her first allowance this week.

4. We (arrive) _____ at the hotel earlier than scheduled.

5. The license plate for my new car (come) _____ in the mail in the next two weeks.

MEMORY TIP

This table summarizes how a verb is conjugated in **simple tense**.

Present	verb	I talk. She talks.
Past	verb + *-ed*	I talked. They talked.
Future	*will* + verb	I will talk. He will talk.

The Perfect Tense

The **perfect tense** shows actions happening <u>before</u> a specific time in the past, present, or future.

> He <u>has finished</u> his homework on time for several weeks.
>
> He <u>had finished</u> his homework on time until he got sick.
>
> By the time he graduates, he <u>will have finished</u> over a thousand home-work assignments.

Perfect tense adds a helping verb to the past tense or **past participle** of the verb. **Past participle** is the grammatical label for the *–ed* form of the verb formed by adding *–d* or *–ed*, to the base form of regular verbs and an *–en* or *–n* ending to the base form of irregular verbs.

> I have <u>ended</u> my vacation.
>
> I have <u>stolen</u> the cash.
>
> After this month, I will have <u>saved</u> a thousand dollars.

Notice that it takes more than one word to show action in the sentences above. In fact, a verb may consist of as many as three words. Taken as a unit, these words form a **verb phrase**.

 MEMORY TIP

A verb phrase is made up of a main verb and one or more **helping verbs**. With the perfect tense, the helping verbs to use are as follows:

	Present	Past	Future
I	have	had	will have
You	have	had	will have
He/she/it	has	had	will have
We	have	had	will have
They	have	had	will have

Present Perfect

The **present perfect** tense shows that an action begun in the past has continued until now; it can also show that an action has just happened. Words like *never, ever, not yet, so far, up to now, just, always, already, before, since, and for years,* and *several times* are often used with the present perfect tense to further describe the action. These words are not verbs but words or adverbs that signal the present perfect tense.

> **MEMORY TIP**
>
> Inserting *never, ever, not yet, so far, up to now, just, always, already, before, since, and for years, several times,* or adverbs in the middle of a verb phrase does not affect the tense or change the form in any way. Chapter Eight explains these adverbs.
>
> I have <u>just</u> finished my homework.
> He has <u>always</u> enjoyed his day off from work.

You use the present perfect to:

- Describe a past experience.

  In my youth, I have visited France.

- Talk about change that has happened over a period of time.

  You have grown since the last time I saw you.

- Indicate accomplishments of humanity or individuals.

  Our daughter has learned to drive.
  Scientists have studied other planets.

- Suggest an action is not complete and more actions are possible.

  I have dealt with many problems so far while working on this project.

To construct the present perfect verb tense, follow this formula:

have or *has* (depending on the subject doing the action) + <u>past participle</u>

I have finished my homework.
He has enjoyed his day off from work.

Past Perfect

The past perfect tense shows an action that has happened <u>before</u> another action in the past. Adverbs like *before* or *prior to* are often used with the past perfect tense. To construct the past perfect tense, use this formula:

had + <u>past participle</u>

The class <u>had finished</u> the project long before the bell rang.

Future Perfect

The **future perfect** tense expresses that something will occur before another action in the future. It can also show that something will happen by or before a specific time in the future. Adverbs like *before* or *by* are often used with future perfect tense.

To construct the future perfect verb tense, use the following formula:

$$\boxed{will\ have\ +\ \underline{past\ participle}}$$

I <u>will have finished</u> my chores by the time my day ends.

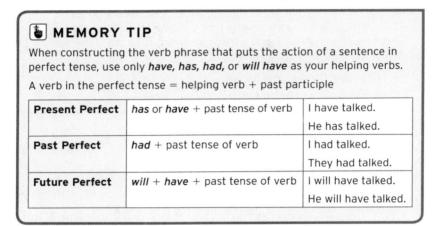

✋ MEMORY TIP

When constructing the verb phrase that puts the action of a sentence in perfect tense, use only *have, has, had,* or *will have* as your helping verbs.

A verb in the perfect tense = helping verb + past participle

Present Perfect	*has* or *have* + past tense of verb	I have talked.
		He has talked.
Past Perfect	*had* + past tense of verb	I had talked.
		They had talked.
Future Perfect	*will* + *have* + past tense of verb	I will have talked.
		He will have talked.

BUILDING SKILLS 2-8: Perfect Tense

Fill in the blank with the verb form in parentheses.

Example: By the time he comes home from work, she (cook) <u>will have cooked</u> dinner. (*future perfect*)

1. Since I have known you, I (enjoy) _____ our friendship. (*present perfect*)

2. The class _____ already _____ (analyze) that book last week. (*past perfect*)

3. Since getting her undergraduate degree, she (specialize) _____ in political anthropology. (*present perfect*)

4. By next week, the Smiths (buy) _____ a new house. (*future perfect*)

5. By tomorrow night, it (snow) _____ three feet more. (*future perfect*)

6. For their engagement, Tom (buy) _____ his girlfriend gold earrings. (*present perfect*)

7. She (work) _____ in advertising for one year before she was promoted. (*past perfect*)

8. Before spring comes, Jim (spend) _____ his entire yearly salary. *(future perfect)*

9. Clare _____ always _____ (do) her work on time. *(present perfect)*

10. By end of this week, I (find) _____ my lost cell phone. *(future perfect)*.

11. The students (discuss) _____ the Shakespeare play since it was assigned as class work. *(present perfect)*

12. By the time they came home, the food left on the table (become) _____ stale. *(past perfect)*

13. Before turning 40 years old, she (had) _____ three children. *(past perfect)*

14. The employees (find) _____ it easy to work with the new computer system. *(present perfect)*

15. By the end of the show, the dancer (danced) _____ three dances. *(future perfect)*

The Progressive Tense

The **progressive tense** shows actions happening continuously, now, in the past, or in the future. The progressive verb tense follows this form:

> Helping verb *to be* + <u>present participle</u>

Just like a past participle, the **present participle** is the grammatical label for the *–ing* form of the verb. A present participle takes the *–ing* ending for all regular and irregular verbs; if the verb ends in *–e,* the *e* is dropped when adding *–ing* like so:

Talk → Talking   Create →Creating

 MEMORY TIP

The verb *to be* is the helping verb for the progressive tenses. It is conjugated like this:

	Present	Past	Future
I	am	was	will be
You	are	were	will be
He/she/it	is	was	will be
We	are	were	will be
They	are	were	will be

Present Progressive

The **present progressive** tense shows action that is continuously in progress right now. In English, *now* can mean this second, today, this month, this year, this century, and so on. Sometimes, you use this tense to say that you are in the process of doing a longer action; however, you might not be doing it at this exact second.

> I am studying to be a nurse.

Sometimes, you may use this tense to indicate that something will or will not happen in the near future.

> She is meeting her friends at the new club.

The present progressive also uses words such as *always* or *constantly* to express the idea that something irritating or shocking often happens.

> They are always coming to class late.

Adverbs or adverb phrases like *now, currently, at this moment, this week*, or *this month* are commonly used with the present progressive verb tense to signal when something is happening. To construct the present progressive verb tense, use the following formula:

> present tense of the verb *to be* (*is, am, are*) + <u>present participle</u>

> Right now, I am reading this interesting book.
> Right now, he is reading his essay.
> Right now, we are reading our papers aloud.

Past Progressive

The **past progressive** tense shows action that is continuously in progress in the past. Use this verb tense to indicate that a longer action in the past was interrupted. Adverbs or adverb phrases like *yesterday at this time* or *when this happened* are often used with the past progressive verb tense. To construct the past progressive verb tense, use the following formula:

> past tense of the verb *to be (was, were)* + <u>present participle</u>

> Yesterday at 2 P.M., I was cleaning my room.
> They were painting the wall when the fire started.

Future Progressive

The **future progressive** tense shows action that will be continuously in progress at a future time. Use this verb tense to indicate that a longer action in the future will be interrupted by a shorter action in the future. Adverbs or adverb phrases like *tomorrow morning* and *this time tomorrow* are frequently used with this verb tense. To construct the future progressive verb tense, use the following formula:

> future tense of the verb *to be* (*will be*) + <u>present participle</u>

I will be working on the project this time tomorrow.
I will be sleeping when she arrives home tonight.

👆 MEMORY TIP

A verb in the progressive tense = verb *to be* + present participle of verb

Present Progressive	*is, am*, or *are* + present participle of verb	I am talking He is talking.
Past Progressive	*was* or *were* + present participle of verb	I was talking. They were talking.
Future Progressive	*will* + *be* + present participle of verb	I will be talking.

BUILDING SKILLS 2-9: Progressive Tense

Underline the appropriate progressive tense.

Example: This time tomorrow, I (will work, <u>will be working</u>) at my new job.

1. Right now, Kevin (is taking, takes) a much needed nap.
2. I (was sleeping, slept) when the rain started falling.
3. By this time tomorrow, she (will be painting, will paint) her room.
4. This Friday, we (are going, go) out to dinner.
5. I (was sitting, sat) down to dinner when the doorbell rang.
6. At this moment, my boyfriend (is thinking, thinks) about his mistake.
7. By the time Doug is in college, he (will be thinking, will think) about what to major in.
8. Greg (was walking, walked) when he was hit by the motorcycle.
9. Finally, the baby (is sleeping, sleeps) soundly.
10. This time next year, we (will be skiing, will ski) on the snow-capped mountain.

The Perfect Progressive Tense

The **perfect progressive tense** is a combination of both the perfect tense and the progressive tense, and it indicates action that has continuously been happening before another action happens, happened, or will happen. Perfect progressive tense requires the use of combining a helping verb—*has, have, had, will have*—with the word *been* and the present participle (*–ing*) of the verb.

Present Perfect Progressive

The **present perfect progressive** tense shows action that has been continuously happening up to the present moment. Use this verb tense to show that something started in the past and has continued up until now. *For five minutes, for two weeks,* and *since Monday* are all durations which can be used with the present perfect progressive tense. The present perfect progressive has the meaning of *lately* or *recently*. To construct the present perfect progressive verb tense, use the following formula:

> *have* or *has* + *been* + <u>present participle</u>

I have been cleaning my room for the last six hours.

Past Perfect Progressive

The **past perfect progressive** tense shows action that has been in progress continuously up to the point of another action in the past. This tense is related to the present perfect progressive; however, the duration does not continue until now because it stops before something else in the past. Using the past perfect progressive before another action in the past is a good way to show cause and effect. The words *when, since, until,* or *for* are often used with this verb. To construct the past perfect progressive verb tense, use the following formula:

> *had* + *been* + <u>present participle</u>

I had been driving on my own when I started ridesharing.

Future Perfect Progressive

The **future perfect progressive** tense shows action that will be in progress continuously up to the point of another action in the future. The words *before, when,* or *for years* are often used with future perfect progressive. To construct the future perfect progressive verb tense, use the following formula:

> *will have* + *been* + <u>present participle</u>

I will have been washing dishes for one hour before you will come home.

> ## 👆 MEMORY TIP
>
> A verb in the perfect progressive tense = helping verb+ **been** + present participle
>
> | Present Perfect Progressive | *has* or *have* + *been* + present participle | I have been talking. He has been talking. |
> |---|---|---|
> | Past Perfect Progressive | *had* + *been* + present participle | I had been talking. |
> | Future Perfect Progressive | *will* + *have* + *been* + present participle | I will have been talking. |

BUILDING SKILLS 2-10: Perfect Progressive Tense

Change the verbs in these sentences to perfect progressive. Write the sentences on the provided lines.

Example: Gina helps me with homework.

Present: <u>Gina has been helping me with homework.</u>

Past: <u>Gina had been helping me with homework.</u>

Future: <u>Gina will have been helping me with homework.</u>

1. Tom talks to me about the navy.

   Present: _____

   Past: _____

   Future:_____

2. Mrs. Johnson asks me about her cat.

   Present: _____

   Past: _____

   Future:_____

3. Mack wishes he were more careful with his artwork.

   Present: _____

   Past:_____

   Future: _____

➡

4. Lance nags Sophia to buy him a new car.

Present: _____

Past:_____

Future:_____

5. David buys his weekly groceries from Savings R Us.

Present:_____

Past:_____

Future:_____

Table 2.1 Verb Tense Round-Up

	PRESENT	PAST	FUTURE
Simple	I play	I played	I will play
Perfect	I have played	I had played	I will have played
Progressive	I am playing	I was playing	I will be playing
Perfect Progressive	I have been playing	I had been playing	I will have been playing

BUILDING SKILLS 2-11: Conjugate Verbs

Conjugate the following verbs.

	Present	Past	Perfect	Progressive
Example: Cry	cry	cried	have/has/had cried	is/am/are/was/were crying
1. plan				
2. refuse				
3. make				
4. serve				
5. receive				
6. paint				
7. convince				
8. marry				

itch				
10. wish				
11. laugh				
12. spend				
13. fish				
14. drag				
15. leave				
16. take				
17. keep				
18. shine				
19. ask				
20. swim				

● BUILDING SKILLS TOGETHER 2-1: Explain
▌ Differences in Tense Meaning

Each pair of sentences is grammatically correct. In small groups, identify the tense used in each sentence. Then explain the difference in meaning between the sentences in each pair.

Example: The bus arrived at 8:00.

The bus will have arrived at 8:00.

Tenses Used: <u>Past, Future Perfect; In the first sentence, the action occurred once and ended. In the second sentence, the action will be completed in the future before another action will be completed.</u>

1. Peter lived in Colorado for three years.

Peter has lived in Colorado for three years.

Tenses Used:_____

_____

_____

2. Was she working?

   Had she been working?

   Tenses Used:_____

   _____

   _____

3. As of December 31, they will have awarded new scholarships twice this year.

   As of December 31, they will be awarding new scholarships twice this year.

   Tenses Used:_____

   _____

   _____

4. Have the directions been explained clearly?

   Had the directions been explained clearly?

   Tenses Used:_____

   _____

   _____

5. She attends the fitness club.

   She has been attending the fitness club.

   Tenses Used:_____

   _____

   _____

REGULAR AND IRREGULAR VERBS

You have learned the twelve verb tenses and may have seen the spelling of a verb change according to the tense in which it is being used. Regardless of verb tense, in English there are two main types of verbs: regular and irregular.

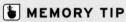 **MEMORY TIP**

The key factor in determining whether a verb is regular or irregular is in identifying its **past tense** or **past participle**.

Regular Verbs

Regular verbs are predictable and follow a clear pattern as they shift tenses. Regular verbs take an *–ed* ending in past tense and in past participle, and the spelling of the base form of the verb itself generally does not change and follows a regular pattern as it goes through the twelve tenses. The past tense and past participle of regular verbs end in *–ed*.

Present	Past	Past Participle
work	worked	have worked

 MEMORY TIP

If the verb can take an *–ed* in simple past tense, the verb does not change in its base form; therefore, it is called a **regular verb**. Table 2.2 lists some common regular verbs.

Tricky Situations with Regular Verbs

There are three tricky situations with spelling regular verbs in other tenses. First, verbs that end in *–e* add a *–d* only in the past and perfect tenses.

decide   not *decideed*   but *decided*

Second, verbs that end in *–y* drop the *–y* and add *–ied* in the past and perfect tenses.

cry   not *cryed*   but *cried*

Third, some verbs that end in a consonant double the last letter before adding *–ed* in the past and perfect tenses.

knit   not *knited*   but *knitted*

Table 2.2 Regular Verb Forms

PRESENT	PAST	PAST PARTICIPLE (HAVE/HAS/HAD)
answer	answered	**(have/has/had)** answered
cry	cried	**(have/has/had)** cried
consider	considered	**(have/has/had)** considered
decide	decided	**(have/has/had)** decided
finish	finished	**(have/has/had)** finished
happen	happened	**(have/has/had)** happened

Table 2.2 Regular Verb Forms (Continued)

learn	learned	(**have/has/had**) learned
like	liked	(**have/has/had**) liked
love	loved	(**have/has/had**) loved
need	needed	(**have/has/had**) needed
open	opened	(**have/has/had**) opened
start	started	(**have/has/had**) started
want	wanted	(**have/has/had**) wanted

BUILDING SKILLS 2-12: Past Tense of Regular Verbs

On the line, write the past tense of each verb in parentheses.

Example: To impress her with his intelligence, he (talk) <u>talked</u> about his research project.

1. To conserve energy, they (turn) _____ off every light in their house.

2. To improve my swing, I (practice) _____ golf in the afternoons.

3. The wind was fierce, so they (wait) _____ for the storm to end.

4. Virginia cooked the meal, and Henry (wash) _____ the dishes.

5. The kittens (look) _____ frail and neglected.

6. Sue (play) _____ the flute last year.

7. Raoul (fish) _____ all day yesterday, but he did not catch anything.

8. For the last week, my mother (work) _____ late at the office.

9. Alyssa (bake) _____ cookies for last night's recital.

10. Last Wednesday, a kind technician (fix) _____ our television.

👆 MEMORY TIP

The simple past tense determines if a verb is regular or irregular.

	Present	Past	Perfect
Regular verb	I open	I opened	I have opened (-**ed** ending)
Irregular verb (new spelling)	I **freeze**	I **froze**	I have **frozen** (changes)

Irregular Verbs

Irregular verbs do not take an *–ed* ending in past tense; instead, the spelling of the base form of the verb itself changes significantly and does <u>not</u> follow a regular pattern as it goes through the twelve tenses. One way to learn these **irregular verbs** is to memorize their spellings or to look them up in a dictionary. Table 2.3 provides a list of some irregular verbs.

Present	Past	Past Participle
sing	sang	have sung

 MEMORY TIP

If the verb **CANNOT** take an *–ed* in simple past tense, the verb changes in its base form; therefore, it is called an **irregular verb.**

Table 2.3 Irregular Verb Forms

PRESENT	PAST	PAST PARTICIPLE (HAS/HAVE/HAD)
am/are/is	was	been
become	became	become
Begin	began	begun
bite	bit	bitten
blow	blew	blown
break	broke	broken
bring	brought	brought
build	built	built
buy	bought	bought
burst	burst	burst
catch	caught	caught
choose	chose	chosen
come	came	come
cost	cost	cost
do	did	done
draw	drew	drawn
drink	drank	drunk

Table 2.3 Irregular Verb Forms (Continued)

drive	drove	driven
eat	ate	eaten
fall	fell	fallen
feed	fed	fed
feel	felt	felt
fight	fought	fought
find	found	found
forget	forgot	forgotten
get	got	gotten
give	gave	given
go	went	gone
grow	grew	grown
have/has	had	had
hide	hid	hidden
hit	hit	hit
hold	held	held
hurt	hurt	hurt
keep	kept	kept
know	knew	known
lay	laid	laid
leave	left	left
let	let	let
lie	lay	lain
light	lit	lit
lose	lost	lost
make	made	made
mean	meant	meant
meet	met	met
pay	paid	paid
put	put	put
quit	quit	quit
read	read	read
ride	rode	ridden
run	ran	run

Table 2.3 (Continued)

say	said	said
see	saw	seen
sell	sold	sold
send	sent	sent
show	showed	shown
shut	shut	shut
sing	sang	sung
sink	sank	sunk
sit	sat	sat
sleep	slept	slept
slide	slid	slid
speak	spoke	spoken
spend	spent	spent
stand	stood	stood
steal	stole	stolen
stick	stuck	stuck
sting	stung	stung
swim	swam	swum
swing	swung	swung
take	took	taken
teach	taught	taught
tear	tore	torn
tell	told	told
think	thought	thought
throw	threw	thrown
understand	understood	understood
wake	woke	woken
wear	wore	worn
win	won	won
write	wrote	written

BUILDING SKILLS 2-13: Irregular Verbs

Read each sentence and underline the appropriate past tense or perfect tense verb.

Example: The lava from the volcano (<u>burst</u>, bursted) unexpectedly.

1. Al had (spoke, spoken) to his father this morning.
2. This morning, the blue jay (sang, sung) beautifully.
3. Lola has (drunk, drank) all her medicine.
4. The new shirt (shrank, shrunk) from being washed in hot water.
5. Bessie (began, begun) taking charge of the situation.
6. Every summer, I have (grown, grewed) tomatoes in my garden.
7. Someone has (stolen, stole) my iPod.
8. The lake (froze, frozen) during the cold winter months.
9. They had (payed, paid) a big price for their new car.
10. Otis (hid, hided) the stolen money in a cookie jar.

Tricky Situations with Irregular Verbs

Some irregular verbs are especially confusing because they change into new words when conjugated. The most confusing irregular verbs are *to be* and *to have*.

Table 2.4 Two Troublesome Irregular Verbs

To Be			
	PRESENT	**PAST**	**PAST PARTICIPLE**
I	am	was	have been
You	are	were	have been
He/she/it	is	was	has been
We	are	were	have been
They	are	were	have been

To Have			
	PRESENT	**PAST**	**PERFECT**
I	have	had	have had
You	have	had	have had
He/she/it	has	had	has had
We	have	had	have had
They	have	had	have had

BUILDING SKILLS 2-14: The Verb *To Be*

Underline the correct verb to complete each sentence.

Example: Three years ago, they (was, <u>were</u>) my biggest financial supporters.
1. Mandy, Brandy, and Cindy (is, am, are) sisters.
2. He (is, am, are) calling for pizza delivery.
3. Yesterday, she (was, were) upset about her math grade.
4. We (has been, have been) on this road for the last six hours.
5. My dress and shoes (is, are, am) in a pile on the floor.
6. The bus (is, are, am) late for its pick-up schedule.
7. This coffee shop (has been, have been) open for three years.
8. You (have been, has been) my friend since third grade.
9. You must always (be, are, is) on time for his class.
10. They (is, are, am) the winners in this competition.

BUILDING SKILLS 2-15: The Verb *To Have*

Underline the correct verb to complete each sentence.

Example: We (has, <u>have</u>) many problems with our new house.
1. The governor of California (has, have) problems with the state budget.
2. We (have had, have) water damage since the last rainstorm.
3. He (has, had) pneumonia last month.
4. I (have, has) some explaining to do about the new locks on the doors.
5. We (have, has) next Monday off as it is a holiday.
6. I (have had, had) nothing but trouble since I bought this old car.
7. Angie and Frank (have, has) no money for their trip.
8. The college (has, have) a new auditorium.
9. Ella and I (have, has) a chemistry test tomorrow, and we are nervous about it.
10. The new house (has, had) four bedrooms and three bathrooms.

Some verbs are so close in meaning and so irregular in conjugation that they are frequently misused and misspelled. *Lie* and *lay*, *rise* and *raise*, and *sit* and *set* are all tricky in this way. Whenever you see or want to use one of these six verbs, ask yourself two questions:

1. What is the exact meaning I intend in this situation?
2. What is the exact time I intend for this action, and what tense is required to express it?

	Meaning	Present	Past	Past Participle
Lie	To take a lying position or to be lying down. Example: **I lie down for a nap every afternoon.**	lie(s)	lay	have/has/had lain
Lay	To put or to place something. Example: **I lay my keys on the desk.**	lay(s)	laid	have/has/had laid
Rise	To go up. Example: **The sun rises in the morning.**	rise(s)	rose	have/has/had risen
Raise	To force something to move up. Example: **She raised the window to let in the fresh air.**	raise(s)	raised	have/has/had raised
Sit	To take a sitting position or to be sitting down. Example: **I sit down in the chair.**	sit(s)	sat	have/has/had sat
Set	To put, to place something Example: **I set the plant by the window.**	set(s)	set	have/has/had set

BUILDING SKILLS 2-16: Lie and Lay

Underline the correct verb for each sentence.

Example: My digital microscope (<u>lays</u>, lies) on top of my scattered science papers.

1. (Lie, Lay) your papers on this table.
2. My brother is sick, so he will (lie, lay) down in bed today.
3. My wallet has (lain, laid) on my desk for the last two days.
4. (Lie, Lay) your head on the pillow.
5. I have (lain, laid) awake until the sun came up.
6. The teacher (lay, laid) his notebook on the podium.
7. James (lain, laid) a bet on the football game.

8. The sun does not (lay, laid) on the horizon very long as it is setting.

9. When you (lie, lay) down after a big meal, you fall asleep quickly.

10. The cleaners (lie, lay) the sheets over the furniture.

BUILDING SKILLS 2-17: Rise and Raise and Sit and Set

Underline the correct verb for each sentence.

Example: He (<u>sets</u>, sits) the alarm clock to wake up at four in the morning.

1. Tom (sits, sets) his iPod in its charging dock station.

2. (Rise, Raise) the flag of the United States of America.

3. We have (risen, raised) our children to be good people.

4. Did you see the smoke (rise, raise) from the chimney?

5. "(Rise, Raise) and shine!" called my sister.

6. The flowers in my garden (raise, rise) their faces to the sun every day.

7. I need to (rise, raise) the bars on my weight machine.

8. We need to (rise, raise) money for the school.

9. The store owner (sits, sets) high prices for the fresh vegetables.

10. The pool's water level (raised, rose) four inches after the heavy rains.

VERB TENSE CONSISTENCY

Although the actions that take place in a story, report, poem, legal document, speech, or letter may show movement between different times, keeping to one tense within each sentence creates clearer writing. Inconsistent shifts in tense can cause confusion. Generally, writers maintain one tense for the main sentence or text and indicate changes in time frame by changing tense relative to that primary tense.

 MEMORY TIP

Do NOT shift tenses within a sentence; make all the verbs in the same tense as the first verb you used in the sentence.

Incorrect: He <u>treats</u> her like a child and <u>is laughing</u> at her when she <u>does</u> something funny.

Correct: He <u>treats</u> her like a child and <u>laughs</u> at her when she <u>does</u> something funny.

OR

He <u>is treating</u> her like a child and <u>is laughing</u> at her when she <u>is doing</u> something funny.

BUILDING SKILLS 2-18: Verb Tense Consistency

Rewrite the following sentences so the verbs are consistent.

Example: He is knowing that he will be cautious when he talked to strangers.

<u>He knows that he is cautious when he talks to strangers.</u>

1. I cut my hair every six weeks because it will be growing too fast.

   _____

2. The flowers are blooming this spring, and I looked forward to their fragrance and beauty.

   _____

3. Missy and I take the same English class, but Missy will have been doing better than I.

   _____

4. Since August, Octavio has planned his trip to Europe, and he will be saving money for it.

   _____

5. The washer and dryer are on sale, and I am affording them at this time.

   _____

◕ BUILDING SKILLS TOGETHER 2-2: Verb Tense Consistency

Working in small groups, underline all the verbs in this excerpt taken from Raymond Carver's *The Bath*; then, change them to present tense. When you have finished changing all the verbs, discuss with your group mates how the text has changed. What have you lost (or gained) by changing the verbs? What verbs did you not change, and why not? The first sentence has been completed for you.

drive

(1) Saturday afternoon the mother <u>drove</u> to the bakery in the shopping center. (2) After she looked through a loose-leaf binder of cake photographs, she ordered chocolate cake. (3) The cake she chose was decorated with a spaceship and a launching pad under a sprinkling of white stars. (4) She asked the baker to ice the name SCOTTY in green as if it were the name of the spaceship. (5) The baker listened thoughtfully when the mother told him Scotty was turning eight years old. (6) He was an older man, this baker, and he wore a curious apron, a heavy thing with loops that went

under his arms and around his back, then crossed in front again where they were tied in a very thick knot. (7) He kept wiping his hands on the front of the apron as he listened to the woman, his wet eyes examined her lips as she studied the samples and talked. (8) He let her take her time. (9) He was in no hurry. (10) The mother decided on the spaceship cake, and then she gave the baker her name and her telephone number. (11) The cake was to be ready Monday morning, in plenty of time for the party Monday afternoon. (12) This was all that the baker said to the woman. (13) No pleasantries and nothing that was not necessary.

—From Raymond Carver, *The Bath*

🕯 BUILDING SKILLS TOGETHER 2-3: Consistent Verb Tense in Writing

Part A: Using complete sentences, in small groups, answer the six questions on the topic of college stress.
Part B: Then, with your group, rewrite the sentences into a paragraph using <u>one consistent</u> verb tense—present, past, or future. You may add more sentences to your paragraph, but be sure to use one specific tense throughout.

Part A

Sentence 1:   Is being a college student stressful?

_____

Sentence 2:   What are some general factors that stress college students?

_____

Sentence 3:   What are some mental or emotional reactions to college stress?

_____

Sentence 4:   What are some physical reactions to college stress?

_____

Sentence 5:   What specific college factor stresses college students the most? Why?

_____

Sentence 6:   How should students cope with that stress? Or what can students do to reduce stress?

_____

Part B
Students and Stress

_____
_____
_____
_____
_____
_____
_____
_____
_____
_____
- -

ACTIVE AND PASSIVE VOICE

Tense is the form of the verb that shows when the subject is performing the action. **Voice** is the form of the verb that shows whether the subject is performing or receiving the action. There are two voices in English: **active** and **passive.**

Active Voice: **Her mom ate the cake.**

Gary drives to campus.

In a sentence with **active voice**, the subject of the sentence performs the action expressed in the verb. In these two examples, _her mom_ and _Gary_ are the subjects performing the verbs _ate_ and _drives_. With the active voice, fewer words are used for a clearer and more direct sentence. In general, clarity and directness are always good qualities to have in your writing, so you may be encouraged to use the active voice whenever possible.

Most action verbs, like _ate_ and _drives_, can also be used in the passive voice. A passive verb is created using a form of _to be_ and the past participle of a given verb (an _–n_ or _–en_ ending to the verb).

Passive Voice: **The cake <u>was</u> eaten by her mom.**

Gary <u>was</u> driven to campus.

In the first example, _her mom_ is still performing the action of eating the cake; yet the words _her mom_ are now the object of the preposition _by_ and not the subject of the sentence. In the second example, the person doing the action is not identified, but _Gary_ is the receiver of the action.

At times, however, the passive voice can be the right choice. It works in the following situations:

- You simply do not know who was responsible for an action.
- You need to be tactful so as not to be hurtful or embarrassing in identifying the subject.
- You do not need to mention the person or thing responsible because it is irrelevant or less important.

Passive Voice: **Da Vinci's *Mona Lisa* was viewed by thousands of art lovers this year.**
It is not important to know who the specific art lovers are in this particular sentence.

 MEMORY TIP

- In the **active voice,** the subject and verb relationship is straightforward: the subject is a **be-er** or a **do-er** and the verb moves the sentence along.

- In the **passive voice**, the subject of the sentence is neither a **do-er** or a **be-er**, but is acted upon by an unnamed someone or something.

BUILDING SKILLS 2-19: Verb Voice

Rewrite the following sentences so the verbs are in active voice.

Examples: The new house was decorated by Marlena.

<u>Marlena decorated the new house.</u>

1. This controversial book was read by Thomas.

   _____

2. The confidential letter was delivered by the kind mail carrier.

   _____

3. The delicious pizza was baked by them.

   _____

4. The fire was started by the broken electric wire.

_____

5. The rude and hurtful comment was made by one of the twins.

_____

BUILDING SKILLS 2-20: Verb Voice

Read this excerpt passage from James Baldwin's Sonny's Blues and identify each verb. Determine the tense of each verb. The first sentence is completed for you.

Simple Past

I <u>read</u> about it in the paper, in the subway, on my way to work. I read it, and I could not believe it, and I read it again. Then perhaps I just stared at it, at the newsprint that was spelling out his name, spelling out the story. I stared at it in the swinging lights of the subway car, and in the faces and bodies of the people, and in my own face, trapped in the darkness, which roared outside.

It was not to be believed and I kept telling myself that, as I was walking from the subway station to the high school. And at the same time I could not doubt it. I was scared, scared for Sonny. He was becoming real to me again. A great block of ice was settling in my belly and all day long, it was melting there slowly while I was teaching my classes in algebra. It was a special kind of ice. It kept melting, sending trickles of ice water all up and down my veins, but it never got less. Sometimes it hardened and seemed to expand until I felt my guts were going to come spilling out or that I was going to choke or scream. This will always be at a moment when I am remembering some specific thing Sonny had once said or done.

When he was about as old as the boys, in my classes his face had been bright and open, there was a lot of copper in it; and he had had wonderfully direct brown eyes, and great gentleness and privacy. I will always be wondering what he may have looked like now. He had been picked up, the evening before, in a raid on an apartment downtown, for peddling and using heroin.

I had kept it outside me for a long time, I had not wanted to know. I had had my suspicions, but I did not name them. I was putting them away all the time. I was telling myself that Sonny was wild, but he was not crazy. And he had always been a good boy, he had not ever turned hard or evil or disrespectful, the way kids can, so quick, so quick, especially in Harlem. I did not want to believe that I will see my brother going down, coming to nothing, all that light in his face gone out, in the condition I had already seen so many others. Yet it happened and here I was, talking about algebra to a lot of boys. . .

—From James Baldwin, *Sonny's Blues*

CHAPTER TWO SKILLS REVIEW: Verbs

Rewrite the following sentences, changing the underlined verbs to the correct tense.

1. It is closed now, but the library open during last summer.

   The library opened last summer

2. Because the computer virus corrupt the whole program, I lose important information, and I was not able to complete the assignment.

3. By the time I left for work, the snow fall heavily on the ground.

   I left for work and it fell heavily on the snow

4. We dance for two hours when the fireworks show began.

   We had danced for 2 hours.

5. Before the day ends, I paint the other side of the house.

   By the day ends will have

6. He bathe the baby when the doorbell rang.

   He bathing the baby when the door bell rang

7. Tomorrow morning, I meet with the general manager about the new job.

   he had watched.

8. The football team play its challenging rivals next Wednesday.

9. After he <u>watched</u> *The Speed Racers,* Trey wanted to drive a fast car.

[handwritten: Trey wanted to drive a fast car after he watched the speed racers]

10. I <u>work</u> for six months by the time I start college this fall.

[handwritten: I worked for six months b/t I started college.]

11. The group of rockers <u>practice</u> for three weeks for this weekend's music contest.

12. We <u>practice</u> our dancing for two weeks before we auditioned for *Dancing Steps.*

13. Ben <u>pass</u> his test before he received his driver's license.

14. He <u>go</u> to his sister's house many times.

15. The director <u>edit</u> the new show now.

CHAPTER THREE: The Third Building Block
Subject-Verb Agreement

In Chapters One and Two, you learned that subjects and verbs are the two major building blocks of a sentence and of English grammar as a whole. However, these two basic elements must agree with each other for the sentence to be effective and clear. Think of two little boys dividing a bag of candy between them. If one boy takes one piece, the other boy will take one piece; if one boy takes two pieces, the other boy will take two pieces. As long as the number of pieces taken by one boy matches the number of pieces taken by the other boy, they are happy—if not, get ready for a fight! The basic elements of a good sentence require a similar agreement. Learning to make subjects and verbs agree is the third building block of grammar. This agreement is most apparent when the verb is in simple present tense, because that is the only verb tense that requires an *s* ending with the pronouns *he*, *she*, or *it*.

SUBJECT-VERB AGREEMENT

Because subjects and verbs must be present in every grammatically complete sentence, they have a strong relationship with one another, especially in simple present tense. When the two elements do not agree, the sentence stumbles, as in these examples:

Dogs is my favorite animals.
Jim eat a hamburger nearly every day.
One of the most precious resources in the United States are water.

MEMORY TIP

The subject-verb agreement is most apparent when the verb is in simple present tense because that is the only verb tense that requires an *-s* ending when the subject is singular or can be replaced with the subject pronouns *he, she,* or *it.*

I walk.	We walk.
You walk.	They walk.
He/she/it walks.	

What exactly is the disagreement between the subject and verb in these sentences? The subject and verb disagree in **number**. A word that refers to one person or thing is **singular** in number. A word that refers to more than one is **plural** in number.

Singular: dog, car, this, each, either, he, she, it
Plural: dogs, cars, these, both, they

 MEMORY TIP

Number in English is determined by using the following subject pronouns to replace the subject:

If the subject can be replaced with *he, she,* or *it* → its number is **singular.**
If the subject can be replaced with *we* or *they* → its number is **plural.**

Rules for Subject-Verb Agreement

In order to agree, a verb must follow the form of its subject in number.

1. **If the subject is singular, the verb must be singular.** An effective test to tell if the subject is singular would be to see if you could replace the noun with a singular pronoun like *he, she,* or *it.*

   My brother (play, plays) football.

   My brother can be replaced with the pronoun *he*. Therefore, *brother* is singular, and the verb that agrees with the subject pronoun *he* is *plays*.

   Correct: My brother <u>plays</u> football.

2. **If the subject is plural, the verb must agree with it.** An effective test to tell if the subject is plural would be to see if you could replace the noun with a plural pronoun like *we* or *they*.

> My brothers (play, plays) football.

My brothers can be replaced with the pronoun *they*. Therefore, *brothers* is plural, and the verb that agrees with the subject pronoun *they* is *play*.

> Correct: **My brothers** <u>play</u> **football.**

To be successful at subject-verb agreement, it is helpful to understand the various forms that singular and plural subjects come in and to consider the verb endings or changes needed for correct subject-verb agreement.

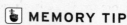 **MEMORY TIP**

Singular subjects can be:
1. Simple singular nouns
2. Collective nouns
3. Words or phrases showing amounts
4. Indefinite pronouns

Plural subjects can be:
1. Simple plural nouns
2. Compound nouns
3. Indefinite pronouns

Singular Subject Rules

1. **Simple and singular nouns.** A sentence can have one singular noun as the subject. This single noun can be replaced with any of the singular pronouns or *he/she/it*. For subject-verb agreement, locate the subject and check to see if it can be replaced with the singular pronouns *he/she/it*.

   > A student (talk, talks) during the lecture.

   He or she talks. Therefore, *A student talks* is the correct answer.

2. **Collective nouns.** Recall that collective nouns name groups composed of members, usually people or things. A collective noun is a single *thing* or *unit* made up of *more than one person* like army, group, or committee. The members of the unit usually function as a singular unit and can be replaced by the pronoun *it*. Test by replacing the collective noun with the pronoun *it*.

   > The team (play, plays) well tonight.

   It plays. Therefore, *The team plays* is the correct answer.

3. **Words or phrases that state amounts.** Some subjects express periods of time, fractions, weights, measurements, quantity, and amounts of money.

MEMORY TIP

Although collective nouns usually function as a singular entity, they can also act individually.

The group acting as one **singular entity** is replaced with the pronoun *it*:

> The group discusses the research findings.
>
>   **It**

The group acting as **individuals** replaced with the pronoun *they*:

> The members of the group discuss the research findings.
>
>   **They**

These subjects are usually singular or act as one thing or as a single unit that can be replaced with the subject pronoun *it*.

> **Six dollars (cover, covers) the price for the movie ticket.**

It covers. Therefore, *six dollars covers* is the correct answer.

> **Half an hour (seems, seem) too long when you are at the doctor.**

It seems. Therefore, *half an hour seems* is the correct answer.

> **Two pounds of potatoes (sits, sit) in the pantry.**

It sits. Therefore, *two pounds sits* is the correct answer.

> **Three-fourth of the painting (shows, show) the artist's muse.**

It shows. Therefore, *three-fourth of the painting shows* is the correct answer.

4. **Indefinite pronouns.** Indefinite pronouns are pronouns that refer to a less clearly identified noun. Indefinite pronouns that end in *-one,-body,* or *-thing* are always singular. For subject-verb agreement, locate the subject indefinite pronoun and test by replacing it with the singular pronouns *he/she/it*.

> **Each student (explain, explains) the meaning of the song.**

He or she explains. Therefore, *Each student explains* is the correct answer.

 MEMORY TIP

The most common indefinite singular pronouns that are replaced with *he/she/it* are:

anybody	nobody	somebody	everybody
anything	nothing	something	everything
anyone	no one	someone	everyone
each	either	neither	none

BUILDING SKILLS 3-1: Verb Agreement with Singular Subjects

Underline the subject and circle the verb that agrees with the subject in each sentence.

Example: The class (go, (goes)) on a field trip.

1. Ed (chooses, choose) clear goals for his life.
2. Susan (understand, understands) the meaning of the word *ubiquitous*.
3. The committee (gather, gathers) every Monday and Wednesday.
4. Everyone in school (longs, long) for the long semester to end.
5. The jury (examines, examine) the evidence in the civil case.
6. The team (plays, play) with more spirit when the stadium is packed with fans.
7. Each of my children (practice, practices) playing on a musical instrument.
8. The New Wave band (perform, performs) the opening act at the concert.
9. Each club member (check, checks) in at the front desk before being admitted.
10. Every Halloween, the child (go, goes) trick or treating.

Plural Subject Rules

1. **Simple and plural nouns.** A sentence can have one plural noun or subject that can be replaced with the pronouns *we* or *they*. For subject-verb agreement, test the subject by replacing it with the plural pronouns *we* or *they*.

   The students (complain, complains) about their assignments.

   We complain. They complain. The students complain.

2. **Compound nouns.** A sentence can have two or more subjects that can be replaced with the pronouns *we* or *they*. Test by replacing with the plural pronoun *they*.

   The students and the teacher (discuss, discusses) the story's theme.

   They discuss. The students and the teacher discuss.

3. **Plural indefinite pronoun.** The indefinite pronouns that are plural in number are: *several, few, both, many*. Test by replacing any of them with the plural pronouns *we* or *they*.

   Many (work, works) the graveyard shift.

   We work. They work. Many work.

> **👆 MEMORY TIP**
>
> The indefinite pronouns *all, any, more, most, none*, and *some* can be singular or plural, depending on how they are used. They are singular when they refer to the <u>quantity</u>. They are plural when they refer to a <u>number</u>.
>
> | | |
> |---|---|
> | <u>Some</u> of the juice is spilled. | (quantity) |
> | <u>Some</u> of the invoices need to be mailed. | (number) |
> | <u>Most</u> of the music is nice to hear. | (quantity) |
> | <u>All</u> of the cake is eaten. | (quantity) |
> | <u>All</u> of the pictures are lost. | (number) |

BUILDING SKILLS 3-2: Verb Agreement with Plural Subjects

Underline the subject and circle the verb that agrees with the subject in each sentence.

Example: <u>Apple pie and ice cream</u> ((go), goes) well together.

1. My thoughts often (become, becomes) confused when I sit down to write an essay.
2. Some of my friends (work, works) on the weekends for more money.
3. Phil and Boris (want, wants) to buy a new computer for their new business office.
4. Both baseball pitchers (make, makes) more money from product endorsements.
5. When it is hot and humid, my clothes (stick, sticks) to me.
6. A computer course and a reference guide (offer, offers) necessary skills for video game players.
7. Mothers (like, likes) to see their children grow into independent adults.
8. Some boys (pitch, pitches) with one hand and (bat, bats) with another.
9. Video editing and computer graphics (provide, provides) new business possibilities.
10. The manager and sales clerk (try, tries) to convince them to buy the expensive video model.

Subject Agreement and Regular and Irregular Verbs

Recall that a regular verb is one whose base form does not change as it moves through the verb tenses. For example:

Present	Past	Past Participle
paint	painted	have painted

In subject-verb agreement, the regular verb will not change its spelling but will take an *-s* ending if the subject is singular or can be replaced with the pronouns *he, she,* or *it.*

Present Tense	
I	paint
You	paint
He/she/it	paints (the spelling of the verb did not change but *-s* is the verb ending)
We	paint
They	paint

To be successful at subject-verb agreement, always locate the subject first, determine its number, then, judge whether the regular verb agrees with it in present tense. If the subject is singular, the verb should generally have an *-s* added to match its singular form with its subject. If the subject is plural (often ending in *-s*), the verb should match its plural form by not adding an *-s.*

🖲 MEMORY TIP

Singular Subject → Verb with *-s*   The **contractor** build**s** the house.

Plural Subject → Verb without *-s*   The **contractors** build the houses.

BUILDING SKILLS 3-3: Subject Agreement with Regular Verbs

Circle the verb that agrees with the subject in each sentence.

Example: The supervisors at my work always (monitor, monitors) our performance.

1. Jack and Lyn (want, wants) to join the new choir group.

2. Teenagers (prefers, prefer) music lessons to math lessons.

3. Cheryl, Sue, and Marissa (belong, belongs) to the same volleyball club.

4. Many of Roger's friends (have, has) football practice every day.

5. I find it funny that Todd and his nephew (is, are) professional house painters.

6. The sugar cookies in the oven (is, are) for this afternoon's tea party.

7. Every week, my nieces and their mother (have, has) lessons in martial arts.

8. The doctors in this clinic (bring, brings) hope to their patients.

9. Stress and nightmares (keep, keeps) me from sleeping at night.

10. Bill and Chris (is, are) good soccer players.

While the base form of a regular verb does not change as it moves through the tenses, the base form of an irregular verb may change, sometimes into completely different words. The most troublesome irregular verbs for subject-verb agreement are *to be*, *to do*, and *to have*. Look at the box here and notice how they change with the pronouns *he*, *she*, or *it*.

Irregular Verb Subject-Verb Agreement		
To be	**To do**	**To have**
Present	**Present**	**Present**
I am	I do	I have
You are	You do	You have
He/she/it is	**He/she/it does**	**He/she/it has**
We are	We do	We have
They are	They do	They have

Those three irregular verbs change completely in present tense if the subject is singular or if the subject can be replaced with the pronouns *he/she/it*. Consider the following examples with the verb *to be*:

Simple Subjects:
Singular subject
↓
The son (is, are) late for the meeting with the lawyer.
Plural subject
↓
The sons (is, are) late for the meeting with the lawyer.

Compound Subjects:
Compound subject
↓
The father and the son (is, are) late for the meeting with the lawyer.

Collective Noun:
Collective noun acting as a single unit
↓
The family (is, are) late for the meeting with the lawyer.
Collective nouns acting as individuals
↓
The members of the family (is, are) late for the meeting with the lawyer.

Indefinite Pronoun:
Indefinite pronoun-singular
↓
Everyone (is, are) late for the meeting with the lawyer.
Indefinite pronoun-plural
↓
All the family members (is, are) late for the meeting with the lawyer.

BUILDING SKILLS 3-4: Subject Agreement with *To Be, To Have,* or *To Do*

Circle the verb that agrees with the subject in each sentence.

Example: She (has, have) a test this week.

1. He (does, do) what he can to help his struggling friends.
2. Six balls (is, are) enough for the tennis game.
3. The trusty mechanic (has, have) replaced the worn brake pads on my car.
4. The group (is, are) finished with the chemistry project.
5. This week, Norma (has, have) three final exams.
6. A bag of groceries (is, are) sitting on the kitchen counter.
7. Each student (has, have) the wrong book for class.
8. The crowd (is, are) angry with the politician at the podium.
9. Somebody (is, are) guilty of the crime of theft.
10. Society (has, have) exact standards for behaving in professional settings.

TRICKY SITUATIONS IN SUBJECT-VERB AGREEMENT

Sometimes, the arrangement of words in some sentences can make it difficult to locate the subject and verb to make them agree. It may be helpful to know the four tricky situations; then, you will know how to determine what to do.

 MEMORY TIP

An easy way to spot prepositional phrases is to consider that such phrases begin with a preposition and end with a noun or pronoun.

Preposition   Preposition
↓   ↓
Into the building → noun   After her → pronoun

Sentences That Start with Prepositional Phrases

Prepositional phrases are words that indicate location, time, or source (take the time to learn and recognize the prepositions listed in Appendix A), but they do not and cannot include the subject of the sentence.

To find the subject in a sentence with a prepositional phrase, consider crossing out the prepositional phrase and looking for the noun or pronoun that remains.

> Outside the wall (walk, walks) an armed guard.

> ~~Outside the wall~~ (walk, walks) an armed guard.

An armed guard can be replaced by *he.*

> He <u>walks</u> outside the wall.
>
> Outside the wall <u>walks</u> an armed guard.
>
> Poisonous ferns (grows, grow) along the winding road to the red house.

Poisonous ferns can be replaced by *they.*

> Poisonous ferns <u>grow</u> along the winding road to the red house.

👆 MEMORY TIP

There are many, many prepositions; some of the most common are listed here:

Place		Time	Source	
above	across	after	about	against
among	around	before	at	by
below	behind	during	because of	due to
beneath	beside	until	except	for
between	beyond	since	from	of
by	in/into	off	to	
inside	near	toward	with	
out	outside	without	here	
over	on			
through	under			
up	upon			
within				

An easy way to help you remember prepositions is to think of the expression *the house*. Then put as many prepositional words as you can in front of the words *the house*:

above the house	**from** the house
around the house	**with** the house
by the house	**to** the house

Sentences Starting with *Here, There, What, Where, When,* **and** *Why*

Here, there, what, where, when, how, and *why* can never be the subjects in the sentences because they are location or preposition words or words related to questions. For location words, reverse the sentence, so you can find the subject and verb. For questions, answer the question in a full statement, then locate the subject and verb.

Here (comes, come) my friend.
Reverse: My friend (comes, come) here.
My friend can be replaced with *he* or *she*.
Here <u>comes</u> my friend.

Here (comes, come) my friends.
Reverse: My friends (comes, come) here.
They come here.
My friends <u>come</u> here.

There (is, are) my book.
Reverse: My book (is, are) there.
My book can be replaced with *it*.
My book <u>is</u> there.
There <u>is</u> my book.

There (is, are) my books.
Reverse: My books (is, are) there.
My books can be replaced with *they*.
My books <u>are</u> there.
There <u>are</u> my books.

Where (is, are) my book?
Answer Statement: My book (is, are) on the desk.
My book can be replaced with *it*.
My book <u>is</u> on the desk.
Where <u>is</u> my book?

Where (is, are) my pens?
Answer Statement: My pens (is, are) on the desk.
My pens can be replaced with *they*.
My pens <u>are</u> on the desk.
Where <u>are</u> my pens?

Why (is, are) my document on the desk?
Answer Statement: My document (is, are) on the desk.
My document can be replaced with *it*.
My document <u>is</u> on the desk because I put it there.
Why <u>is</u> my document on the desk?

Why (is, are) my books on the desk?

Reverse: My books (is, are) on the desk because I put them there.

My book can be replaced with *they*.

My books <u>are</u> on the desk because I put them there.

Why <u>are</u> my books on the desk?

BUILDING SKILLS 3-5: Subject-Verb Agreement with Prepositional Phrases, and *Here, There, What, When, Where, How,* and *Why*

Circle the verb that agrees with the subject in each sentence.

Example: Underneath the plastic cover ((sleeps), sleep) the drunk man.

1. There (is, are) a light shining through the woods.
2. What (is, are) the recipe for this cake?
3. During the hottest part of the day and under the big tree (sits, sit) a group of children.
4. When (is, are) the party guests arriving?
5. When (is, are) the party guest arriving?
6. Here (is, are) the keys to that new convertible car.
7. The receipts from the shoe store (is, are) in my wallet.
8. The receipt from the shoe store (fit, fits) in my wallet.
9. There (is, are) two important financial decisions to be made.
10. Why (does, do) the dishwasher beep at the end of each cycle?
11. At the end of my workday (comes, come) a sense of completion.
12. Near the top of the hill (sits, sit) a restaurant with a view of the countryside.
13. Annie, where (do, does) these letters go?
14. In the sick man's eyes, there (is, are) peace and acceptance.
15. At the back of the theater (stands, stand) two ushers.

Sentences with *Either/Or, Neither/Nor,* and *Or*

When you have a sentence that includes *either/or, neither/nor,* or *or,* be sure to locate the subject that is closer to the verb to determine what happens to the verb.

Either the students or the teacher (talk, talks) about the bad test.

Teacher is the subject closest to the verb, and it can be replaced with *he/she*; then, the correct answer is:

> **Either the students or the <u>teacher talks</u> about the bad test.**

> **Either the student or the teachers (talk, talks) about the bad test.**

Teachers is the subject closes to the verb and it can be replaced with *they*; then, the correct answer is:

> **Either the student or the <u>teachers talk</u> about the bad test.**

The same would apply to *neither/nor* but here is what it looks like with *or*:

> **The students or the teacher (talk, talks) about the bad test.**

The teacher can be replaced with *he/she*.

> **The students or the <u>teacher talks</u> about the bad test.**

 MEMORY TIP

An easier way to remember interrupters may be by using the word *scoopables*. Scoopables refer to the non-essential information between two commas that separates the subject and the verb.

subject   *verb*

↓   ↓

Tom, <u>the next-door neighbor,</u> is an agent with the Federal Bureau of Investigation.

If you removed the scoopable, the sentence is still clearly understood.

> **Tom is an agent with the Federal Bureau of Investigation.**

Sentences with Interrupters

Interrupters could be a word or a group of words that appears between the subject and verb, but these words are not important to the basic meaning of the sentence and "interrupt" the structure of the sentence. When the interrupters are "scooped out" or removed from the sentence, the sentence still makes perfect sense. The nonessential information that comes between the subject and verb must be put between commas.

> **The students, not the teacher, (talk, talks).**

The students, ~~not the teacher,~~ (talk, talks).

The students can be replaced with *they*.

The students, not the teacher, <u>talk</u>.

Harry, not his cousins, (win, wins) at the horse races.

Harry, ~~not his cousins,~~ (win, wins) at the horse races.

Harry can be replaced with *he*.

Harry, not his cousins, <u>wins</u> at the horse races.

BUILDING SKILLS 3-6: Subject-Verb Agreement with *Either/Or* and Interrupters

Circle the verb that agrees with the subject in each sentence.

Example: Eugene, the one who teaches biology and chemistry, (ⓘ**s**, are) sick today.

1. Neither John nor his teachers (have, has) a solution to his dilemma.

2. Quentin, the captain of three teams, (is, are) going to have knee surgery.

3. Either stress or pain from my legs (keeps, keep) me awake at night.

4. The old house, the one owned by the Ramseys, (stands, stand) behind the grove of orange trees.

5. My brother or my sister (takes, take) the dog for his daily walk.

6. Al, despite all his friends and admirers, (remains, remain) a lonely man.

7. Either the rose bushes or the lemon tree (fits, fit) in that spot in the yard.

8. Either the rose bushes or the lemon trees (fits, fit) in that spot in the yard.

9. Your friends, the ones who know your sister, (parties, party) too hard.

10. The wine stewards, not Robert, (recommend, recommends) this white wine.

11. He claims that neither employer (spend, spends) much money on bonuses.

12. The swimmers or the coach (needs, need) to see the videotape from the last meet.

13. Harold, one of the lawyers, (selects, select) the cases carefully.

14. The girl across the street or the boys around the corner (play, plays) in the empty parking lot.

15. Nora, one of the talented skiers, (falls, fall) hard down the slope.

BUILDING SKILLS 3-7: Subject-Verb Agreement in Writing

Write the subject on the first line and the correct verb on the second line.

Example: Children (is, are) affected by the images they see in various media.
>   Children <u>are</u>

1. Television (is, are) a common fixture in American homes. _____ _____

2. Violence on television (concerns, concern) many parents. _____ _____

3. Here, the term *violence* (refer, refers) to use of physical force against another person. _____ _____

4. On average, the American child (spends, spend) 20 to 25 hours each week watching TV. _____ _____

5. Children's cartoons (has, have) one violent act every three minutes. _____ _____

6. Before reaching adolescence, the average North American youngster (see, sees) several thousand murders on TV. _____ _____

7. What (is, are) the impact of this steady diet of televised violence? _____ _____

8. A child, according to social cognitive theory, (learn, learns) by observing others and imitating what she or he sees. _____ _____

9. These researchers (predict, predicts) more aggressive behavior from children who are exposed to violent TV. _____ _____

10. In the end, the aggressive behaviors may either (put, puts) them behind bars or (ruin, ruins) their interactions with others. _____ _____

–Adapted from Kail/Cavanaugh, *Human Development: A Life-Span View*

♦ BUILDING SKILLS TOGETHER 3-1: Writing Sentences with Subject-Verb Agreement

Working with a partner, complete the following sentences using subject-verb agreement rules. The sentences have been started for you.

Example: Simple subject:
This campus <u>is abandoned during the summer months.</u>

1. Compound subject:
   The men and women _____

   _____

2. Collective noun:
   This group _____

   _____

3. Indefinite pronoun:
   Somebody_____

   _____

4. Prepositional phrase:
   Into the sky _____

   _____

5. Here/There with a singular subject:
   Here _____

   _____

6. Here/There with a plural subject:
   There _____

   _____

7. Question words:
   Where _____

   _____

8. Either/Or:
   Either he _____, or he _____

   _____

9. Interrupters (or Scoopables):
   With a singular subject:_____

   With a plural subject: _____

   _____

10. Here/There with a plural subject:
    There _____

    _____

◖ BUILDING SKILLS TOGETHER 3-2: Subject-Verb Agreement in Writing

With a partner, read this excerpt, underline the subjects, and circle all the verbs in the passage. Then, using the lines on the next page, change all the verbs to simple present tense being mindful of subject-verb agreement. The first sentence is completed for you.

(1) Her name *was* Connie. [*is*] (2) She was fifteen and she had a quick nervous giggling habit of craning her neck to glance into mirrors, or checking other people's faces to make sure her own was all right. (3) Her mother, who noticed everything and knew everything and who hadn't much reason any longer to look at her own face, always scolded Connie about it. "Stop Gawking at yourself. Who are you? You think you're so pretty?" she said. (4) Connie raised her eyebrows at these familiar complaints and looked right through her mother, into a shadowy vision of herself as she was right at that moment: she knew she was pretty and that was everything. (5) Her mother had been pretty, if you could believe those old snapshots in the album, but now her looks were gone and that was why she was always after Connie. (6) Her sister was twenty-four and still lived at home. (7) She was a secretary in the high school Connie attended, and if that wasn't bad enough—with her in the same building—she was so plain and chunky and steady that Connie had to hear her praised all the time by her mother and her mother's sisters. (8) June did this, June did that, she saved money and helped clean the house and cooked and Connie did not do a thing, her mind was filled with trashy daydreams.

(9) Their father was away at work most of the time and when he came home, he wanted supper, and he read the newspaper at supper and after supper, he went to bed. (10) He did not bother talking much to them, but around his bent head Connie's mother kept picking at her until Connie wished her mother was dead and she herself was dead and it was all over. (11) There was one good thing: June went places with girl friends of hers, girls who were just as plain and steady as she, and so when Connie wanted to do that her mother had no objections. (12) The father of Connie's best friend drove the girls the three miles to town and left them off at a shopping plaza, so that they walked through the stores or went to a movie, and when he came to pick them up again at eleven he never bothered to ask what they did there.

—From Joyce Carol Oates, *Where Are You Going, Where Have You Been?*

1. _____   7. _____
2. _____   8. _____
3. _____   9. _____
4. _____   10. _____
5. _____   11. _____
6. _____   12. _____

CHAPTER THREE SKILLS REVIEW: Subject-Verb Agreement

Circle the verb that agrees with the subject in each sentence.

1. In America, each person (enjoys, enjoy) the right to freedom.

2. Sam, one of Tim's friends, (plays, play) professional tennis.

3. At the end of Esperanza Street (stand, stands) an old and abandoned church.

4. Jonathan (talks, talk) to his mother every day.

5. There (is, are) too many people on this ski lift.

6. Neither the teachers nor the administration (want, wants) a strike.

7. Lucy and George (believe, believes) in hard work.

8. Lucy or George (believe, believes) in hard work.

9. The jury (announces, announce) the decision in the murder case.

10. The murderers (is, are) taken to jail.

11. Here (sits, sit) my grandmother.

12. Neither of the girls (want, wants) to work tonight.

13. May, one of the medical students, (fails, fail) her biology test.

14. There (is, are) many grammar errors in my research paper.

15. Swimming and golf (is, are) my favorite sports.

16. Something (does, do) not look right in this situation.

17. At the back of the book, the pictures (contain, contains) valuable information.

18. The problem of transporting products (is, are) complicated by rising gas prices.

19. Behind the shed and around the oak tree (waits, wait) the scared teenager.

20. Her father, one of the best Army majors, (has, have) an incurable disease.

21. He is a man who (protects, protect) his family.

22. Alex, as well as his relatives, (throws, throw) a summer party.

23. Either Grace or her sisters (present, presents) the flowers to the bride.

24. The union (votes, vote) on the new proposal.

25. Behind the locked doors (lies, lie) a big fortune in gold.

26. Everyone (turns, turn) in today's assignment.

27. Joe, one of the staff members, (understands, understand) the manager's opinion.

28. A dozen (is, are) too many eggs for a little boy to eat.

29. At the other end of the phone line (cries, cry) an anxious mother.

30. The herd of cattle (is, are) killed by mad cow disease.

UNIT TWO: Pronouns

CHAPTER FOUR: The Fourth Building Block
Pronouns

Should you use *who* or *whom* in addressing a letter? Do you say, "Between you and me" or "Between you and I"? Is it "She is nicer than me" or "She is nicer than I"? These examples demonstrate the most frequent problems people have with pronouns. It is important to learn about pronouns—the fourth building block—because they are useful little words that replace nouns in sentences and clarify meaning. For instance, in recounting a story to others, rather than saying "Jim said to Jim's mother, 'Jim failed Jim's driving test,'" you might say, "Jim said to *his* mother, '*I* failed *my* driving test.'" A properly used pronoun will improve the flow of your speaking or writing and will help eliminate awkward and repetitive words.

Pronouns are words that can replace nouns. They allow you to communicate complete thoughts without using exact nouns every time. For example, you can use *him* instead of "Dr. James J. McFarlane," *there* instead of "Washington, D.C.," and *that* instead of "the new shampoo I bought and tossed next to the soap in the bathroom."

Pronouns do not just make your writing or speaking more efficient, but they also help you add variety and appeal. Unfortunately, pronouns are misused almost as frequently as they are used. That is why the fourth building block to correct writing is learning to use pronouns clearly and accurately. This building block relies on your understanding of subjects and verbs.

PRONOUN USAGE

You can use pronouns to reduce repetition of nouns or to clarify the subject(s) in your sentences. Consider this paragraph:

> Jerry came to class. Jerry listened to the teacher's lecture, and Jerry wrote in Jerry's notebook as the teacher talked. Jerry's friend Julie

passed Jerry a note with a question about the lecture. Jerry left when class ended, and went home to study for Jerry's upcoming test.

Now consider this paragraph:

Jerry came to class. He listened to the teacher's lecture, and he wrote in his notebook as the teacher talked. His friend Julie passed him a note with a question about the lecture. He left when class ended, and went home to study for his upcoming test.

Which paragraph sounds better and easier to read? You probably agree that the second paragraph is the better one. The use of the pronouns *he, his,* and *him* in place of the noun *Jerry* helps make the second paragraph sound better. The word *Jerry* is the **antecedent**—the word replaced by all the pronouns *he, his,* and *him.*

Pronouns come in different forms, and it is important to know when to use which form. The form a pronoun takes in a sentence is referred to as **case.** The three kinds of cases are:

1. **Subjective case** where the pronoun takes the place of a subject in the sentence.
2. **Objective case** where the pronoun tells to whom or for whom the sentence's action is done.
3. **Possessive case** where the pronoun shows ownership of something in the sentence.

Here is a chart to show how each case changes a pronoun.

Subjective	Objective	Possessive
I	me	my, mine
you	you	your, yours
he, she, it	him, her, it	his, her, hers, its
we	us	our, ours
they	them	their, theirs

Subjective Case

The pronouns that make up the category of subjective pronouns are:

I/we	they
you	who
he/she/it	

Subjective pronouns are used in place of the subject in a sentence.

MEMORY TIP

Subjective case pronouns often fall <u>before</u> a verb because they perform the verb. They are called subjective pronouns because they fill the "subject" position in a sentence by indicating who or what is doing or being something.

You will need to use the subjective case in the following situations:

1. **The subjective pronoun is at the beginning of the sentence to tell who or what is doing or being something.**

   I dance in the hall.
   He walks down the street.
   We eat our hamburgers.
   They talk about the political situation.

2. **The subjective pronoun is being used after a comparison signal word such as *than* or *as*.** In this arrangement, the pronoun is not at the beginning of the sentence but appears as part of a clause.

 MEMORY TIP

A clause is a group of words with a subject and verb.

Subject Verb
↓   ↓
I drink coffee.

The words *am, are,* and *do,* which complete the clause, have been omitted. Therefore, the pronouns that come after *than* or *as* are subjects of "understood" verbs or verbs that are not visible but implied or inferred.

   She is taller than I.

Notice that this sentence is actually saying: She is taller than *I am.* The *I* and *am* make up the clause. It may sound better to say: She is taller **than me**. However, grammatically, you cannot say: She is taller than **me am**, because the pronoun *me* cannot perform the verb *am*.

   Incorrect: We play better than them. ("them do")
   Correct: We play better than they. ("they do")

3. **The subjective pronoun follows a verb *to be* such as *am, is, are, was, were,* or *will be.***

> Incorrect: I believe the thief is him.
> Correct: I believe the thief is he.

The pronoun *he* comes after the verb *is* and if you reverse the sentence, you would get: He is the thief. We cannot say *him* because that pronoun cannot perform the verb.

> Incorrect: Him is at the door.
> Correct: It is he at the door.   /

BUILDING SKILLS 4-1: Subjective Pronouns

Circle the correct pronoun in parentheses.
Example: Sammy is as shrewd as (her, (she)).

1. She and (I, me) loaded the car for our camping trip.

2. (He, Him) and Nathan always go camping in Big Bear.

3. The murderer in this case was (him, he).

4. My best friends and (I, me) take the same classes in college.

5. The cheerleaders for our team will be (them, they).

6. I should be paid more than (he, him) because I work harder.

7. Jay and (I, me) were chosen for the debate team.

8. It was (she, her) at the marketing conference.

9. It is (she, her) calling you on your cell phone.

10. Marley, Tom, and (I, me) are planning a wedding shower for Stacy.

11. We were just as competitive as (they, them) in bowling.

12. It will be (they, them) who disappear from the party scene.

13. In packaging our merchandise, Mike works faster than (she, her).

14. (Us, We) poor factory workers are always overworked and underappreciated.

15. I was as pleased as (she, her) about the positive results.

Objective Case

The pronouns that make up the category of objective pronouns are the following:

me/us	them
you	whom
him/her/it	

This form of pronoun is needed whenever a pronoun receives the action of the verb or comes after a preposition.

 MEMORY TIP

Objective case pronouns often fall <u>after</u> the verb or preposition because they are *to whom* or *for whom* the verb is being performed. They are called objective because they fill "object" positions. An object to the verb is a word or a group of words functioning as a noun or a pronoun that follows the verb and receives the action of the verb. An object can be:

- **Direct** when it answers the question *what* or *whom* in connection with the verb
  I met Dr. Spencer. (*whom* did I meet?)

- **Indirect** when it answers the question *to whom* in connection with the verb.
  I sent the letter to my supervisor. (*To whom* did I send the letter?)

You will need to use the objective case in the following situations:

1. **The objective pronoun receives the action of the verb**. In this arrangement, the pronoun answers the question *what* or *whom* in connection with the verb.

   I will bring it to your house.   (**What** will I bring? It)

   I saw him at the club.   (**Whom** did I see? Him)

2. **The objective pronoun comes after a preposition.** Prepositions are words that add information by showing time (*before, during, after, . . .*), location (*behind, between, in front of, . . .*), and source (*to, for, from, by, of, about, . . .*). Refer to Appendix A for a complete list of prepositions. When the pronoun is placed after the preposition, it must take the objective form because it answers the question *to whom, for whom, by whom, with whom,* or *from whom* in connection with the verb.

   I gave the letter to him.   (To whom did he give the letter? Him)

   He walked with them.   (With whom did he walk? Them)

3. **The objective pronoun falls after the words** *between* **and** *let's*. *Between* is a preposition showing location, so any pronoun after it should be of the objective case.

> **Between you and me, she is not nice.**

Most commonly, "Between you and I" is used; however, *I* is a subjective pronoun when objective pronouns need to be used after a preposition like *between*. *Let's* is really a contraction of the words *Let* and *us* and means "let us." *Us* is an objective pronoun, so to clarify who the *us* is, you need to use pronouns from the objective case.

> **Let's you and me take a walk in the park.**

It is more commonly heard as "Let's you and I" but that is not correct pronoun use.

BUILDING SKILLS 4-2: Objective Pronouns

Circle the correct pronoun in parentheses.

Example: The contractor called ((her,) she) with the construction estimate.

1. The Nobel Prize was awarded jointly to him and (her, she).

2. Between you and (I, me), I think Ben stole the cash.

3. The contest was judged by John and (I, me).

4. The boss praised (I, me) for the successful completion of the project.

5. Mrs. Jeffries offered her accounting services to (me, I).

6. Yvonne trusted Marybeth and (him, he) to tell the workers about the change in plan.

7. Let's you and (me, I) go tell the neighbors about the snake.

8. It was hard for (we, us) to work on the building plans.

9. The singer gave a special performance for Louise and (him, he).

10. Between me and (her, she) is the big issue of deception.

11. Sam gave Tracy and (her, she) a ride to the mall.

12. The concert was a disappointment for my sister and (me, I).

13. Dad split the money between my brother and (me, I).

14. The play was boring for (I, me).

15. Let's you and (me, I) organize the closet for the office.

Possessive Case

The pronouns that make up this category are the following:

my, mine	our, ours
your, yours	their, theirs
his, her, hers, its	

This form of pronoun is needed whenever a pronoun is used to show ownership. You will need to use possessive case in the following situations:

1. **The pronoun appears before a noun to show possession.**

    My report on American government is almost done.

    Their suggestions have been very helpful.

2. **The pronoun appears before a verb that is being used as a noun or a gerund.** Some nouns are formed from verbs. These nouns are called gerunds and are formed by adding -ing to a verb to name an activity; for example, *talking, swimming, sewing,* or *smoking.*

    Your smoking is a dangerous habit.

    I did not like his running past me without saying hello.

3. **The pronoun stands alone to indicate possession.**

    That car is theirs, not ours.

    Is this coffee mug yours or mine?

BUILDING SKILLS 4-3: Possessive Pronouns

Underline the possessive pronouns in this passage.

   Sorting out and folding the laundry are major tasks in our house. They probably are in most houses, but in ours, they are a bother! It used to be her—my sister's—job, but last week my mother made it mine. She dropped the laundry basket down in my bedroom doorway and announced that I would be the Laundry Girl for the next two weeks.

   We are a large family. Our family consists of Mother, Dad, the triplets, Alison, Letty, and me. Daily, my mother washes three laundry loads including one just for socks. Mother's socks are easiest to find. Hers are all small and black. Dad's socks are not too hard to spot as his are big and beige or navy-colored. Letty's and Alison's socks are easy to find because theirs are mostly red or pink knee-highs. However, the triplets' socks are hard! Theirs come in all sizes, colors, and types—soccer socks, school socks, baseball socks, and socks for the Scouts. There are so many of them; it takes a long time to sort theirs all out. These days, I dread doing the laundry even sorting and folding what is mine.

OTHER PRONOUNS

Besides the subjective, objective, and possessive cases for pronouns, there are other troublesome kinds of pronouns. It can be difficult to determine which ones to use.

Who vs. Whom

These words are notoriously tricky, along with their companions *whoever* and *whomever*. *Who* and *whoever* are subjective pronouns, so they are always used <u>before the verb</u> as the subject in the sentence.

> <u>Who</u> is at the door?
> He chose <u>whoever</u> volunteered for the English project.

Whom and *whomever* are objective pronouns, so they are always used as the receiver of the verb or after a preposition.

> The student <u>whom</u> I know studies hard will pass the test.
> To <u>whom</u> are you talking?
> You can select <u>whomever</u> you want.

 MEMORY TIP

If you are choosing between *who* and *whom*, look to the right of these words to see the next or immediate word right after. If the next word after *who* or *whom* in a statement is a **verb**, the correct pronoun is the subject and almost always will be *who*.

Verb
↓
The students who <u>study</u> well will pass the class.

If the next important word after *who* or *whom* is a subject (noun or pronoun), the correct pronoun is an object and almost always will be *whom*.

Pronoun
↓
I need one person whom <u>I</u> can rely on.

Noun
↓
Those for whom <u>diabetes</u> is an issue must watch their diets.

BUILDING SKILLS 4-4: Using Who vs. Whom

Circle the correct pronoun in parentheses.
Example: The students ((who) whom) study diligently will pass the math exam.

1. (Who, Whom) does the teacher think is most talented?

2. To (who, whom) does this jacket belong?

3. You have to ask (whoever, whomever) is on duty about the extra towels.

4. You can be sure Kevin knows (who, whom) is at fault in this case.

5. The operator (who, whom) Mrs. Johnson hired left early.

6. To (who, whom) should these invitations be sent?

7. The preacher will talk to (whomever, whoever) will listen.

8. I wonder (who, whom) the love song is about.

9. Everybody in camp (who, whom) got bitten by the mosquitoes was given treatment.

10. The worker (who, whom) used to work here has been fired.

11. Ask (whoever, whomever) you invited to the club to bring drinks.

12. The sailor (who, whom) I was talking to told me about the storm.

13. He mailed the letter to (whoever, whomever) contacted him about the job.

14. Tell (whoever, whomever) is at the front desk that we need the paramedics.

15. Many for (who, whom) diabetes is an issue must watch their carbohydrate intake.

Demonstrative Pronouns

Demonstrative pronouns direct attention to specific people, places, or things. The demonstrative pronouns are:

Singular	Plural
This	These
That	Those

The pronouns *this* and *that* are directed at singular nouns whereas *these* and *those* are directed at plural nouns. Use *this* before singular nouns and *these* before plural nouns to refer to things that are <u>physically close</u> to the speaker in time and place.

   This is for a singular noun near the speaker.

   <u>This</u> piece of paper in my hand is important to my future.

   These is for plural nouns near the speaker.

   <u>These</u> books I am holding are historical.

> **MEMORY TIP**
>
> When *this* is used to begin a sentence, the antecedent is often unclear to the reader.
>
> <u>This</u> is unacceptable.
>
> What is *this* referring to? The noun *this* could be referring to is not identified, so this sentence is unclear.
>
> <u>This</u> lack of respect is unacceptable.
>
> *This* refers to a specific subject: lack of respect, so this sentence is clear.

Use *that* before singular nouns and *these* before plural nouns to refer to things that are physically distant from the speaker in time and place.

That is for singular nouns far from the speaker.

> <u>That</u> piece of paper on my desk over there is trash.

Those is for plural nouns far from the speaker.

> <u>Those</u> books we saw yesterday at the museum are priceless.

BUILDING SKILLS 4-5: Using Demonstrative Pronouns

Circle the correct pronoun in parentheses.

Example: (This, That) house in front of me is the one I want.

1. (This, That) has been a difficult year for the economy.

2. Would you please deliver (this, that) letter on the table over there?

3. (These, Those) shoes I have on are the best shoes I have ever worn!

4. Are we going the right way? Is (this, that) where we parked the car?

5. Bethany donated (those, these) ugly sofas she has at her apartment to the homeless shelter.

6. Chris can work with (those, these) data numbers on customer satisfaction that we have in front of us.

7. Alan finds (this, that) new family situation he is now facing a problem.

8. The answer to (this, that) math problem in our book is not correct.

9. (These, Those) plans we drafted yesterday will work.

10. (These, Those) strawberries from last night's dessert were delicious!

Relative Pronouns

Relative pronouns connect a description of the subject to the subject itself. The pronouns that make up this category are *that, which, who, whom,* and *whose. That* and *which* refer to things.

He found the phone <u>that</u> he had lost.

> (The pronoun *that* = the lost phone)

Linda' math textbook, <u>which</u> costs eighty dollars, is lost.

> (The pronoun *which* = textbook)

👆 MEMORY TIP

- Use *which* to introduce parenthetical material, interrupters, or scoopables—material that can be removed from a sentence without changing the essential meaning of the sentence. A *which* clause is often set off with a comma or a pair of commas.
- Use *that* for material deemed indispensable for the meaning of a sentence. A *that* clause is <u>not</u> set off with commas.

Who and *whom* refer to people.

Her mother, <u>who</u> is wearing the red suit, is the head of the company.
(The pronoun *who* = mother)

Paul, <u>whom</u> we all admire, rides well.
(The pronoun *whom* = Paul)

Whose shows that something belongs to or is connected to something or someone. Do not confuse *whose* with *who's,* which means "who is."

The man <u>whose</u> wife was murdered looked stricken.
(The pronoun *whose* = the man's)

BUILDING SKILLS 4-6: Using Relative Pronouns

Circle the correct relative pronoun in parentheses.
Example: The detective, ((whose) which) work is noted here, is retired now.

1. People (who, whom) are concerned about the economy are spending less money.

2. The Hugo brothers, (whose, which) restaurant burned down, are moving to California.

3. The banking industry, (which, that) suffered great financial losses recently, is floundering.

4. My neighbors buy food (whose, that) is labeled "organic."

5. Henry is one of the lawyers (that, who) works long hours.

6. The award, (which, that) is given to the best actor, went to a movie legend.

7. Some scientists, (whose, which) research has been published, uncover controversial conclusions about different phenomena.

8. The taxes (that, which) Americans pay yearly fund many important transportation projects.

9. Marketers, for (whom, who) trends are important, predict customer buying habits.

10. Leilani, (that, who) is a student at Harvard, is studying neurobiology.

Interrogative Pronouns

Interrogative pronouns are used to begin a question. The pronouns that make up this category are *what, which, who, whom,* and *whose.*

> <u>What</u> is the name of this new fashion trend?
> <u>Which</u> one of the artists died prematurely?
> <u>Who</u> is the prime suspect in this murder investigation?
> <u>Whom</u> do I need to address in this letter of reference?
> <u>Whose</u> car is in our neighbor's driveway?

BUILDING SKILLS 4-7: Using Interrogative Pronouns

Fill in the blanks with the correct interrogative pronoun.
Example: To <u>whom</u> do I give this prize?

1. _____ do you think will preside over the meeting?

2. He asked _____ I preferred juice or coffee?

3. Of _____ child are you complaining?

4. To _____ did the grandmother leave the money?

5. _____ of the two remaining applicants do you want to interview?

6. _____, if anything, did you learn from this experience?

7. _____ money have you taken? You should surrender it now!

8. _____ wrote the Phantom of the Opera?

9. Of all the cities you've visited _____ one did you like best?

10. _____ jacket was left in the Lost and Found bin?

Reflexive Pronouns

Reflexive pronouns end in -*self* and *selves* and "reflect back" or refer to an antecedent (a noun or pronoun) earlier in the sentence. They act as intensifiers, following a noun or pronoun.

> I <u>myself</u> wrote that research paper.
> I wrote that memo <u>myself</u>.

They are also used after verbs or prepositions when the receiver of the action is the same as the subject of the verb in the clause.

> <u>He</u> gave <u>himself</u> a reward.
> Before the meeting, <u>she</u> allowed <u>herself</u> time to focus her thoughts.
> At the end of our two-mile hike, <u>we</u> decided to give <u>ourselves</u> a treat.

In each of these sentences, the reflexive pronouns reflect back to the subject of the sentence and is the receiver of an action verb or a preposition.

Antecedent	Reflexive pronouns
I	myself
You	yourself
He, she, it	himself, herself, itself
We	ourselves
They	themselves

Writers make two types of errors when using the reflexive pronoun form. The most common error is the inappropriate use of a "self" pronoun where a simple pronoun is sufficient. Sometimes, you may use a "self" pronoun for more "elegant" writing, but it actually is wordy and unnecessary.

Incorrect: **The boss invited my wife and myself to an expensive dinner.**
Correct: **The boss invited my wife and me to an expensive dinner.**

The other all-too-common error is the use of misspelled forms of the reflexive pronoun, such as:

Misspelled	Correct
hisself	himself
theirself theirselves	themselves
ourself	ourselves
themself	themselves

If you tend to use any of these forms, consider removing them from your vocabulary as they are unacceptable.

BUILDING SKILLS 4-8: Reflexive Pronouns

Fill in the blanks with the correct reflexive pronoun
Example: He talked <u>himself</u> into agreeing to the other party's offer.

1. Many times I wish that our car would wash _____.

2. On Saturdays, I often wash the car by _____.

3. Sometimes my children clean the car windows by _____.

4. When my children clean the car windows, I say, "Congratulate_____ on doing a wonderful cleaning job."

5. We enjoy the team effort involved in washing the car _____.

PRONOUN-ANTECEDENT AGREEMENT

Just as a verb must agree with its subject, so a pronoun must agree with the noun it replaces. That noun—called the **antecedent**, can be anything, but it will have a recognizable point of view, number, and gender. The pronoun reference has to agree with the <u>person</u>, <u>number</u>, or <u>gender</u> of the antecedent. Pronoun-antecedent agreement happens in three ways:

- Person: the noun's point of view (they, he/she, you, or it)
- Number: singular or plural
- Gender: masculine or feminine

Pronoun Agreement with Person

Here the pronoun agrees with the point of view (which person or what thing) of the antecedent.

👆 MEMORY TIP

The **antecedent** is the word that the pronoun refers to or replaces.

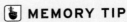 Michael sold his restaurant to an investment company.
        ↓   ↓
Antecedent   Pronoun referring back to Michael

He sold his restaurant to an investment company.
 ↓   ↓
Pronoun   Pronoun

If the antecedent is <u>a person</u>, then agreement can be achieved by using the pronouns *he* or *she*. If the antecedent is about the <u>second person</u> *(you)*, then agreement can be achieved by using the pronoun *you*. If the antecedent is <u>a thing</u>, then agreement can be achieved by using the pronoun *it*.

If <u>a person</u> wants to succeed in this game, <u>he</u> or <u>she</u> must know the rules.
If <u>you</u> want to succeed in this game, <u>you</u> must know the rules.
For <u>this game</u> to be successful, <u>it</u> needs to have specific rules.

👆 MEMORY TIP

Use the same person throughout a sentence. Maintain the point of view that begins the sentence or the text.

Inconsistent: <u>You</u> must be careful when <u>you</u> hike because the consequences could be deadly for <u>him or her</u>.

Consistent: <u>You</u> must be careful when you hike because the consequences could be deadly for <u>you</u>.

Inconsistent: <u>One</u> must always persevere especially in times of hardship because <u>I</u> have to surpass the obstacles to achieve <u>our</u> dream.

Consistent: <u>One</u> must always persevere especially in times of hardship because <u>one or he/she</u> has to surpass the obstacles to achieve <u>one's or his/her</u> dream.

BUILDING SKILLS 4-9: Pronoun Agreement with Person

Rewrite each sentence to correct the errors with pronouns. Be sure to maintain the pronoun point of view for each sentence.

Example: He should know that one must shop around before you buy a car.

He should know that he must shop around before he buys a car.

1. I could feel the sun warming your arms.

_____

2. I enjoy mountain climbing because you use your physical strength.

_____

3. I finally realized that one has to think before you say something.

_____

4. In summer, people want to be outdoors but do not want to do what is needed to protect himself from the harsh sun.

_____

5. The street sweeper starts its route at two o'clock every morning.

_____

6. The ride operator left his customers waiting while they got lunch.

_____

7. She opened a health spa after one finished her career as a medical doctor.

_____

8. People would rather have one's food be tasty than nutritious.

_____

9. He is a well-known personality although some people find me a controversial figure. _____

10. Fast-food chains use artificial flavors for its sauces and dressings.

_____

Pronoun Agreement with Number

The pronoun must agree with the antecedent's number. Number refers to the antecedent's singular or plural state.

If the antecedent is **singular**, the pronouns *he* or *she* or *it* must be used.

If <u>one person</u> wants to succeed in this game, <u>he or she</u> must know the rules.

If the antecedent is **plural**, the pronoun *they* must be used.

If <u>people</u> want to succeed in this game, <u>they</u> must know the rules.

 MEMORY TIP

Number in English is determined by using the following <u>subject pronouns</u> <u>to replace the subject</u>:

If the subject can be replaced with *he, she,* or *it* → its number is **singular.**

If the subject can be replaced with *we* or *they* → its number is **plural.**

TRICKY SITUATIONS WITH PRONOUNS AND NUMBERS

The number agreement is most confusing when a sentence includes a singular indefinite pronoun or a collective noun because writers assume these words are plural when they are, in fact, singular.

Situation One: Singular indefinite pronouns are pronouns that do not indicate a definite person or thing. Here is a list of some common singular indefinite pronouns:

everybody	everyone	everything	each
anybody	anyone	anything	either
somebody	someone	something	neither
nobody	no one	nothing	

Whenever these pronouns are used in a sentence, a singular pronoun (he or she or his or her) is required to refer back to them.

Incorrect: **Someone left <u>their</u> folder behind.**

Correct: **Someone left <u>his or her</u> folder behind.**

Incorrect: **<u>Everyone</u> must turn in <u>their</u> work.**

Correct: **<u>Everyone</u> must turn in <u>his or her</u> work.**

Incorrect: **<u>Each</u> of the boys brought <u>their</u> book.**

Correct: **<u>Each</u> of the *boys* brought <u>his</u> book.**

Presently, some writers and speakers have a tendency to use the plural *their* as the reference pronoun to indefinite pronouns. This seems like an easy way to avoid the historically sexist practice of always using *his* when referring to a general person. However, since these indefinite pronouns emphasize a "single" body, one, or thing, the singular pronouns *he, she, his, her,* or *it* should be used. The best course is to use both pronouns such as *he or she* or *his or her,* as in the previous.

> **MEMORY TIP**
>
> Plural indefinite pronouns, such as *several, few,* and *both,* may require the use of the pronoun *their* as the reference pronoun.

BUILDING SKILLS 4-10: Pronoun Agreement with Indefinite Pronouns

Circle the pronoun that agrees with the indefinite pronoun in bold.
Example: Everyone must turn in ((his or her,) their) group report.

1. **Everyone** was required to write a letter to (his or her, their) mayor.

2. **One** of the doctors at this hospital is liked by (his or her, their) patients.

3. **Each** of the boys is getting (his, their) new car today.

4. **Few** like to have debt that (he or she, they) cannot pay.

5. **Someone** walking by the construction site must watch (his or her, their) steps.

6. **Everybody** living in this house speaks highly of (his or her, their) cook.

7. **Anyone** who wants to bid on the cabin needs to raise (his or her, their) hand.

8. **Many** who conform to society's rules stand to lose (his or her, their) own individuality.

9. **Neither** the boys nor their sister was given (their, his, her) weekly allowance.

10. To **each** (his or her, their) own.

11. **Someone** forgot to turn off (his or her, their) irrigation system.

12. **Several** of the girls gave (her, their) names.

13. **Either** John **or** Bill will present (his, their) findings on the criminal case.

14. **Many** students should do (his or her, their) best when it comes to taking tests.

15. **Neither** of the girls brought (her, their) completed job application.

Situation Two: Collective nouns always require a singular pronoun reference. Collective nouns, such as army, team, or committee, sound plural but in reality are singular entities composed of many elements. For example, a team is a single entity made up of many players. Because it is still a "single" entity, it requires the singular pronoun *it* for reference.

> The <u>army</u> deployed <u>its</u> recruits.
> The <u>team</u> played <u>its</u> final game.

 MEMORY TIP

Although collective nouns usually function as a singular entity, they can also act individually.

> The <u>committee</u> discusses the research findings <u>it</u> received.

The committee acting as one *singular entity* replaced with the pronoun *it*.

> The <u>committee members</u> discuss the research findings <u>they</u> received.

The committee acting *as individuals* replaced with the pronoun *they*.

BUILDING SKILLS 4-11: Pronoun Agreement with Collective Nouns

Insert the right pronoun on the line. The pronoun must agree with the collective noun it replaces.

Example: The jury announced <u>its</u> unanimous decision.

1. The group turned in _____ long report.

2. The board members met about _____ new agenda.

3. The committee had _____ first meeting today.

4. The band mates practiced _____ new musical lineup.

5. The members of the committee shared _____ findings with the city officials.

6. The airplane crew reviewed _____ maintenance procedures.

7. The girls' soccer team had _____ first win.

8. For two hours, the teammates worked hard on _____ game strategy.

9. The board of directors finally gave _____ recommendation regarding the company.

10. The gang members plotted _____ attack on the rival gang.

> ### 🖐 MEMORY TIP
>
> To keep your pronouns in agreement with their numbers, remember:
>
> When a pronoun refers to a **plural noun**, use *their*.
>
> > The cats ate <u>their</u> treats.
>
> When a pronoun refers to an **indefinite pronoun**, use *his or her*.
>
> > Everyone shares <u>his or her</u> story.
>
> When a pronoun refers to a **collective noun**, use *it* or *its*.
>
> > The group talks about <u>its</u> research progress.

Pronoun Agreement with Gender

A pronoun has to agree with the masculine or feminine state of the antecedent. When a pronoun refers to a <u>singular female noun</u>, the pronoun must be gender-specific (she, her).

> The <u>girl</u> turned in <u>her</u> assignment.

When a pronoun refers to a <u>singular male noun</u>, the pronoun must be gender-specific (he, his).

> The <u>man</u> walked <u>his</u> dog.

BUILDING SKILLS 4-12: Pronoun Agreement with Gender

Rewrite the following sentences to correct the errors in pronoun use.

1. He could taste the cake crumble in his mouth, and they did not want the feeling to end.

   _____

   _____

2. The little girl lost his doll.

   _____

   _____

3. The man quickly decided that they would attend the party.

_____

_____

4. Her plants need to be watered; they have been on vacation, and no one from the office has watered them.

_____

_____

5. The congressional representative gave their support to the loyal mayor candidate.

_____

_____

◖ BUILDING SKILLS TOGETHER 4-1: Writing with Pronouns

With a partner, refer to a popular YouTube video and practice writing sentences about it using the different types of pronouns. On the lines next to each type of pronoun, write two sentences about the video being sure to use each listed pronoun.

Subjective

_____

_____

_____

_____

Objective

_____

_____

_____

_____

Possessive

_____

_____

_____

_____

Who and Whom

_____
_____
_____
_____

Demonstrative Pronouns

_____
_____
_____
_____

Relative

_____
_____
_____
_____

Interrogative

_____
_____
_____
_____

Reflexive

_____
_____
_____
_____

Pronoun Agreement with Person

_____
_____
_____
_____

Pronoun Agreement with Number

_____

_____

_____

_____

Pronoun Agreement with Gender

_____

_____

_____

_____

❚ BUILDING SKILLS TOGETHER 4-2: Pronouns
❚ in Writing

Working with a partner or in a small group, read this passage and correct all pronoun errors. Write the correct answer over the error.

(1) Gods and great heroes have long been important to Hindus. (2) The stories of gods have been told to children to help him and her learn about our religion and about the values he should live by. (3) One of these stories is of Princess Savitri, the only daughter of King Asvapathi. (4) Her was a charming, clever, and noble young woman whom had fallen in love with a fine-looking young man named Satyaban. (5) Satyaban was the son of a hermit or a person whom lives by themselves away from others. (6) Hermits are honored among Hindus for there great wisdom. (7) Everyone in the kingdom wanted to agree to the match, but they worried about a princess's ability to live the tough life of a hermit. (8) To help their King stop Savitri from marrying Satayaban, Narada, Satyaban's father, told them that the enemy has put a curse on his son: within a year of your marriage Satyaban would die. (9) Savitri learned of the terrible curse but her insisted on marrying Satyaban. (10) The King granted your wish.

(11) The couple lived in harmony until Satyaban suddenly died on the day that marked a year from our wedding. (12) The king of the dead, Yama, came to claim Satyaban, but Savitri held on to himself and would not let go. (13) Yama was surprised by the young wife's devotion to his husband and told them he would grant

them any wish but that for the life of her husband. (14) Savitri asked for 100 sons with Satyaban. For Yama to make this possible, they had to bring back Satyaban from the dead since Satyaban could not have children unless it was alive. (15) He restored the young man's life and from that day on Savitri became a model to all young women. (16) Herself showed the power and goodness of love and the importance of having a clever side.

BUILDING SKILLS TOGETHER 4-3:
Pronouns in Writing

Working with a partner or in a small group, read this passage and correct all pronoun errors. Write the correct answer over the error.

(1) Right there right there in the middle of the field him says himself wants to put that thing together. (2) Him and his buggy ideas and so me says "how you gonna get it down to the water?" but him just focuses me out with him eyes rolling like they do when himself gets into some new lunatic notion and him says not to worry none about that. (3) Just would I help him and because himself don't know how you can get it done in time otherwise. (4) Though you'd have to be loonier than him to say yes me says me will of course help. (5) I always would. (6) Crazy as my brother is I have done little else since me was born and mine wife she says "I can't figure it out I can't see why you always have be babying that old fool him isn't never done nothing for you. Yourself got enough to do. Fields here need plowing it's a bad enough year and now that red-eyed brother of yours winging around like a cloud and not knowing what in the world him is doing building a boat in the country. What next?"

(7) It is not a fishing boat him wants to put up; it is the biggest thing I ever heard of and for weeks us did nothing but cut down pine trees and haul them out to his field which is pretty high up a hill. (8) Mine wife she sighs and says crazy am me and her four months with a child and trying to do mine work and hers too and still when I come home from hauling timbres all day, she rub me shoulders and back.

(9) The days pass and mine brother says us have to work harder and from time to time he gets neighbors to come give a hand but them do not stay around

more than a day or two and them go away shaking their heads disgusted they got weaseled into the thing in the first place.

(10) We get the thing done all finished, and I come home on that last day and I say to mine wife "I'll be home all the time now." (11) One day I get an idea, so I go over to my brother's place for some wood left over from building the boat and I see them are all living on that boat in the middle of nowhere him and his boys and wife.

(12) The next day, it's raining and we stay inside and do things around the place and us are happy because the rain has come just in time. (13) The rain never stopped and after a week of rain, the crops are ruined and water it stands around in big pools with the house getting full of water. (14) So I set out to my brother's houseboat and nobody comes out to let I in. (15) I turn around and head back for home but the rain is thundering and I can't make it no further so I head to a hill and collapse at the top of it. (16) I look out and see my brother's boat is floating and I wave at it but don't see nobody wave back and I look at me own place and all I see is the top of it. (17) Tearing for the house swimming most all the way was me but the rain still coming down. (18) I can't see my brother's boat no more. I can't see my house no more. (19) I left me wife inside where I found she. (20) I could not hardly stand to look at she the way her was. (21) How did he know?

CHAPTER FOUR SKILLS REVIEW: Pronouns

Circle the correct answer.

1. My brother and (I, me) share a small bedroom.

2. The child baked a cake for (you and me, you and I).

3. May I speak with Tony? Yes, this is (he, him).

4. The party at fault in this accident is (he, him).

5. Even the jury was shocked by (its, their) decision.

6. My sister buys food (whose, that) is labeled "gluten-free."

7. The computer belongs to Tom and (she, her).

8. The father is shorter than (they, them).

9. Martha finds (this, that) the current family situation she is now facing is problematic.

10. The banking industry, (which, that) suffered great financial losses recently, is floundering.

11. It was (he, him) who left her crying at the party.

12. The boss gave raises to my friends and (I, me).

13. The committee just published (its, their) condemning report.

14. Either the girls or the boy will speak to (their, his) mother.

15. Mrs. Brent is the counselor (who, whom) you can talk to if you have a problem.

16. The ones who are sorry are (they, them).

17. (This, That) book is the national best seller.

18. Let's keep this a secret between you and (me, I).

19. (He and she, Him and her) are going to get married.

20. Everyone knows that (he/she, they) must turn in (his/her, their) test on time.

21. He is as short-tempered as (her, she).

22. Is this the person (who, whom) I should speak to?

23. We overwhelmed (themselves, ourselves) with stress before our residential move.

24. The one who has sacrificed the most is (she, her).

25. The team has won most of (its, their) games.

UNIT THREE: Clauses and
Kinds of Sentences

CHAPTER FIVE: The Fifth Building Block
Clauses

What can you do with building blocks? You can stack and balance blocks of various shapes and sizes to construct towers, bridges, buildings—even whole towns. You have already learned that a subject and verb are the required building blocks for a complete sentence, and that those two elements must agree with each other in person, number, and gender. In the next few chapters, you will explore correct ways to build complicated and more elaborate sentences using **clauses** or groups of words that contain subjects and verbs. Clauses are essential tools to achieve variety in sentence structure and to engage the reader in your writing.

CLAUSES

A **clause** is a group of words containing a subject and verb. A clause may express a complete thought when the group of words is an **independent clause,** or it may express an incomplete thought when the group of words is a **dependent clause.**

It is important to understand the difference between a sentence and a clause. Both are grammatical labels for a group of words that must contain a subject and a verb. A sentence <u>may</u> contain more than one subject/verb groups; in other words, a sentence may consist of one, two, or more clauses. Regardless of the number of clauses a sentence has, it always expresses a complete thought.

> ✋ **MEMORY TIP**
>
> A clause = Subject + Verb → <u>may or may not</u> express a complete thought.
> Sentence = Subject + Verb → expresses a complete thought and may
>   contain several clauses.

To find how many clauses a sentence has, consider breaking it down into separate clauses by underlining the subject (noun or pronoun) and verb (action or state of being) in each group of words or clause.

| I own a beautiful cat. | Number of clauses: 1
Number of sentences: 1 |
| I own a beautiful cat; her fur is glossy black, and after I brush it, her eyes glow with pleasure, and she snuggles in my arms with loud purrs of contentment. | Number of clauses: 5
Number of sentences: 1 |

In underlining the subject (noun or pronoun) and verb (action or state of being) in each clause, you can see the number of clauses each sentence has.

I own a beautiful cat	complete thought
her fur is glossy black	complete thought
after I brush it	incomplete thought
her eyes glow with pleasure	complete thought
she snuggles in my arms with loud purrs of contentment	complete thought

BUILDING SKILLS 5-1: Identifying Clauses in Sentences

Read each sentence and underline the subject (noun or pronoun) and circle the verb (action or state of being) in each clause. On the line next to each sentence, write the number of clauses you have identified.

Example: _____2_____ He (is) our new neighbor, but he (is) very eccentric.

_____ 1. His cyber life is much more exciting than his real life.

_____ 2. Conducting research teaches students how to formulate questions and how to find answers.

_____ 3. She was not interested in staying in school; she moved to Columbus, Ohio.

_____ 4. She is known to most people as Madonna, and her real name is Madonna Louise Veronica Ciccone.

_____ 5. Thirteen people set out to get help; five survived, and two returned and helped rescue the trapped relatives.

_____ 6. Some people are fearful of purchasing items with food preservatives because they feel these chemicals may cause cancer.

_____ 7. My bowling ball is special; it is red and purple, and it is decorated with little bumblebees for good luck.

_____ 8. The violent serial killer was captured by the police and imprisoned for life.

_____ 9. Although it is not the most powerful memorization strategy by itself, repeating information out loud helps.

_____ 10. Many of us have a love-hate relationship with technology; we love the convenience but hate the dependence.

Types of Clauses

There are two types of clauses:

- Independent
- Dependent

Learning to recognize the difference between independent and dependent clauses will help you create and punctuate complex sentences without confusing your reader. Just as you need to learn how to balance and place blocks of differing size, shape, and weight, so, as the writer, you must learn how to arrange and connect clauses of differing completeness and purpose.

Independent Clause: A Clause That Makes Sense on Its Own

An **independent clause** (IC) contains a subject and a verb and expresses a complete thought. As its name suggests, an independent clause is a complete sentence that can stand by itself and does not need more information to give it meaning.

> **Dan laughed.**

Dan is the subject and _laughed_ is the verb. Do you need to know more? Not really. You might want to know what made Dan laugh, where he is and who he is with, or whether his laugh was happy or bitter—but these pieces of information are not essential for understanding what the sentence means. Answers to these questions might shed more light on Dan and his laughter, but grammatically, all that matters is that the sentence has a subject and a verb and that it makes sense on its own. _Dan laughed,_ therefore, is an independent clause.

MEMORY TIP

Independent Clause = Subject + Verb → Complete Thought

Dependent Clause: A Clause That Requires More Information to Make Complete Sense

A **dependent clause (DC)** has a subject and a verb but does not express a complete thought. As its name suggests, a dependent clause is *dependent on* more information to give it meaning. It cannot stand on its own as a complete sentence.

> When Dan aughs.

Although *Dan* is the subject and *laughs* is the verb, you need to know more to make a complete statement. What happens when Dan laughs? Does someone smile or get mad at him? Do other people join him? You need more information to complete the meaning of this clause. Adding another clause will provide the needed information:

> When laughs, the walls shake, and the baby wakes up from his nap.

When Dan laughs, therefore, is a dependent clause.

 MEMORY TIP

Dependent Clause = Subject + Verb → **Not** a Complete Thought

Notice that the **dependent clause** in the example above was created by the addition of an opening word (*when*) which told the reader to wait for additional information. *When* is one of a group of words called **subordinating conjunctions.** Learning this group thoroughly will help you to see if a clause is independent or dependent, complete or incomplete.

 MEMORY TIP

Use the acronym WASBIT to help you memorize the most common subordinating conjunctions:

W	**W**hen, **W**here, **W**herever, **W**henever, **W**hereas, **W**hether, **W**hile
A	**A**s, **A**s if, **A**s long as, **A**s though, **A**lthough
S	**S**ince, **S**o that
B	**B**efore, **B**ecause
I	**I**f
T	**T**hough

Whenever you see a word from the list above at the beginning of a sentence, expect to find at least two clauses in the sentence. Create long, interesting sentences in your own writing by adding a word from this list to the beginning of an independent clause, then write a second clause—or more!—to continue and to complete the thought.

To sum up, both independent and dependent clauses are important for good writing. An independent clause anchors every sentence with sturdy completeness. A dependent clause offers variety and suspense, often preparing the reader for an important action (*the baby wakes*) or surprising them with unexpected details (*the walls shake*). Chapter Six, Kinds of Sentences, will help you learn more about combining clauses.

BUILDING SKILLS 5-2: Identifying Independent and Dependent Clauses

Read each sentence and determine if the clause is independent or dependent. On the line, write *IC* for independent clause or *DC* for dependent clause.

Example: Because I failed my math test.   <u>DC</u>

1. When you have finished reading that history book.   _____

2. Car dealers are offering new ways to buy cars.   _____

3. Until the long fall semester is over.   _____

4. The cold blizzard struck the small village unexpectedly.   _____

5. When I was a Red Cross volunteer in 2003.   _____

6. Pelican birds gracefully glide and soar over the ocean's water.   _____

7. She received a letter of warning from the federal court.   _____

8. If we reach our intended destination by nightfall.   _____

9. He completed his elaborate artwork for the museum.   _____

10. Although November 13th was a sunny warm day.   _____

11. I believe in freedom for all humankind.   _____

12. If this weak economy ever gets better.   _____

13. The jackpot winners were congratulated by the casino manager.   _____

14. The mysterious psychic predicted the big earthquake in California.   _____

15. Swimming is an excellent way to burn calories. _____

16. As the graceful deer scrambled for safety. _____

17. We arrived just in time for the alternative rock concert. _____

18. Because we were stuck in snarly traffic. _____

19. The president's speech made us hopeful of what is to come. _____

20. Because eggs are a good source of protein. _____

BUILDING SKILLS 5-3: Writing Independent and Dependent Clauses

Change the following dependent clauses to independent clauses.

Example: When the race was cancelled.

        <u>The race was cancelled.</u>

1. After Timothy ate the well-prepared dinner.

    _____

    _____

2. When the sun came up.

    _____

    _____

3. Before the stage curtain opens.

    _____

    _____

4. As I danced to the exhilarating music.

    _____

    _____

5. Before she left for her trip to Europe.

    _____

    _____

6. When he missed the biology test.

    _____

    _____

7. While they plotted for the practical joke on Alicia.

_____

_____

8. Although we wanted to go fly-fishing.

_____

_____

9. While you were away from home.

_____

_____

10. Until the newly decorated basket was filled with candy.

_____

_____

First, change the following sentences to dependent clauses, then add an independent clause to explain or complete the dependent clause.

Example: The soup tasted delicious.
    <u>Although the soup tasted delicious, it was too hot to eat quickly.</u>

11. James rode his new bike to work.

_____

_____

12. He left to go to Lake Superior.

_____

_____

13. The weather was cold in December.

_____

_____

14. Emily walked home alone.

_____

_____

15. Cynthia is going to town to pick up some fruit for the afternoon picnic.

_____

_____

16. The college administration has decided to raise faculty salaries.

_____

_____

17. Board games are fun for the entire family.

_____

_____

18. The economic recession increased the unemployment rate.

_____

_____

19. The waterfall was the best feature at the Raging Waters park.

_____

_____

20. The professional soccer team gathered on the field.

_____

_____

BUILDING SKILLS 5-4: Writing Independent and Dependent Clauses

Describe the room you are in at this moment. Write at least five sentences that contain dependent clauses and that answer many of the following questions:

1. Where are you located at this moment? What room are you in?

2. What do you see around you or in front of you?

3. What colors surround you? What do you think of the colors?

4. What do you hear? Why?

5. What does the sound remind you of or make you feel?

6. What do you smell? Why?

7. What do you touch? How does it feel? What does it make you think of?

8. Do you taste anything? Do you like what you taste? Why?

9. Overall, how do you feel about the room you are in at this moment?

10. Would you recommend that others visit this room?

_____

_____

_____

_____

_____

_____

_____

_____

Once you have completed writing your sentences, underline the independent clauses you have used and circle the dependent clauses.

🖊 BUILDING SKILLS TOGETHER 5-1: Clauses in Fiction

Read this excerpt from Louise Erdrich's *The Red Convertible*. Working with a partner, underline the independent clauses, and circle the dependent clauses.

(1) I was the first one to drive a convertible on my reservation. (2) It was red, a red Olds. (3) I owned that car along with my brother Henry Junior. (4) We owned it together until his boots filled with water on a windy night and he bought out my share. (5) Now Henry owns the whole car, and his youngest brother Lyman (that's myself), walks everywhere he goes.

(6) How did I earn enough money to buy my share in the first place? (7) My own talent was I could always make money. (8) I had a talent for it, unusual in a Chippewa. (9) From the first I was different that way. (10) Everyone recognized it. (11) I was the only kid they let in the American Legion Hall to shine shoes, for example, and one Christmas I sold spiritual bouquets for the mission door to door. (12) The nuns let me keep a percentage. (13) Once I started, it seemed the more money I made the easier the money came. (14) Everyone encouraged it. (15) When I was fifteen I got a job washing dishes at the Joliet Café, and that was where my first break happened.

(16) It was not long before I was promoted to bussing tables, and then the short-order cook quit and I was hired to take place. (17) No sooner than you know it I was managing the Joliet. (18) The rest is history. (19) I went on managing. (20) I soon became part owner, and of course there was no stopping me then. (21) It was not long before the whole thing was mine.

(22) After I had owned the Joliet for one year, it blew over in the worst tornado ever seen around here. (23) The whole operation was smashed to bits. (24) A total loss. (25) The fryalator was up in a tree, the grill torn in half like it was paper. (26) I was only sixteen. (27) I had it all in my mother's name and I lost it quick, but before I lost it, I had every one of my relatives, and their relatives, to dinner, and I also bought that red Olds I mentioned along with Henry.

—From Louise Erdrich, *The Red Convertible*

CHAPTER FIVE SKILLS REVIEW: Clauses

In each sentence of the following paragraph, underline the independent clause and circle the dependent clause.

1. When the bell rang, the boys dashed out of class.

2. When they got home, they packed their camping gear.

3. They wanted to get to Lake Arrowhead before the sun set.

4. After they got to the lake, they set up their tent.

5. Jim started the campfire while Ben prepared the dinner.

6. The boys were hungry because they had not eaten since school let out.

7. After they ate, they shared ghost stories.

8. As they lay in their sleeping bags that night, they could hear the rain come down.

9. They were frightened by the wind howling through the trees.

10. They knew it would be a while before they fell asleep.

CHAPTER SIX: The Sixth Building Block
Kinds of Sentences

Human beings love repetition, rhythm, and pattern—and humans equally love variety and surprise. This double love is always at work in almost everything we build, including parks, bridges, towns, or landmarks. Learning the rules for combining clauses will strengthen your ability to build language that creates rhythm and variety in everything you write.

In writing, you produce different sentences based on combining independent and dependent clauses into various arrangements. Combining clauses can give your writing flexibility, clarity, and strength.

> **📠 MEMORY TIP**
>
> ■ When a clause makes full and complete sense by itself, it is called an **independent clause**.
>
> ■ When the clause requires more information to make full and complete sense, it is called a **dependent clause**.

If not combined logically and punctuated clearly, however, clauses will create ineffective sentences that will bring confusion to your reader. This chapter introduces four different kinds of sentences—**simple, compound, complex,** and **compound-complex**—and explains how to connect and punctuate each one.

SIMPLE SENTENCES

A sentence that has **one independent clause** and no dependent clause is called a **simple sentence**.

I ate cake.

MEMORY TIP

Simple Sentence = One Independent Clause (IC)

A simple sentence never has more than one clause, but that clause may contain compound subjects and verbs.

T.J. and Richy ate all the cake.

Mona and the kids finished off the punch and cookies.

Everybody cleared the dishes, turned off the lights, and locked the door.

BUILDING SKILLS 6-1: Writing Simple Sentences

Write five simple sentences using the subjects listed below.

Example: My car <u>is an old grey sedan with a broken trunk latch.</u>

1. My friend _____

2. Last night, I _____

3. The lake water _____

4. My desk _____

5. This class _____

Many writers rely heavily on using simple sentences because these sentences are easier to manage grammatically or because they do not know how to create new combinations. However, overreliance on simple sentences can result in paragraphs like this:

My mother never got a chance to go to college. She struggled all her life to make a good living. She worked two jobs in order to make ends meet. She dreamed of her children going to college. My mother saved money for her children's education. She has two children in college now. She is very proud of us. My mother worked hard to see her children become educated.

What do you notice is happening in this paragraph? Even though the subject, *my mother*, is replaced occasionally by the pronoun *she*, every sentence in this paragraph has

1. a single clause of one type (independent),
2. a single arrangement of the major parts of speech (subject then verb), and
3. a single length (subject + verb + one descriptive phrase).

Taken all together, the lack of variety in this group of sentences makes the writing boring, choppy, and unnaturally stiff. It does not convey the passion of a son or daughter celebrating a mother's accomplishments. Now consider this version:

> My mother never got a chance to go to college because she struggled all her life to make a living. Nevertheless, she dreamed of her children getting the chance she never had, so for years she worked two jobs to save money for their education. My mother has two children in college now. She is extremely proud of them, but we are prouder of her, for it is her hard work that has allowed us to become educated.

How does this version sound? Do you think it is smoother and more passionate? Although the first paragraph is made up of simple sentences, the second paragraph features different kinds of sentences with multiple clauses for a more flowing, vivid style. The number of sentences has been reduced from eight to four, but the complexity of those four sentences conveys more information and emotion than all eight did in the earlier version. Notice that the second paragraph still contains a simple sentence: "My mother has two children in college now." Placed in the midst of more complex sentence structures, this straightforward statement carries emotional weight. It is important to practice writing all types of sentences, for each can play a powerful role in your own compositions.

 MEMORY TIP

In writing paragraphs, essays, research papers, business reports, or even electronic memos, <u>avoid the overuse of simple sentences</u>. To create interesting writing that will keep the reader engaged with your ideas, <u>join clauses</u> and vary your sentence patterns.

SENTENCE VARIETY

To vary sentence patterns and create exciting sentences, we combine clauses. When independent clauses are combined, a **compound sentence** is produced. When one independent and one dependent clause are combined, a **complex sentence** is produced. When multiple independent and dependent clauses are combined, a **compound-complex** sentence is produced.

To combine clauses, use **conjunctions** and **punctuation** (primarily semicolons and commas). Conjunctions are words that join or link together clauses. They also indicate the relationship between the ideas expressed in the clauses.

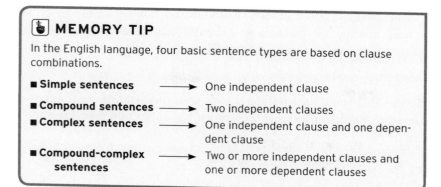

Joining Independent Clauses: Compound Sentences

A **compound sentence** contains two or more independent clauses. Each clause, when viewed alone, can stand on its own as a sentence without changes or additions. In the English language, the term *compound* refers to a combination of two elements. When you combine two independent clauses together, you produce a compound sentence like so:

I ate cake | and | my girlfriend ate cookies .
Independent clause   *Independent clause*

There are three ways to join two independent clauses and to create a compound sentence:

1. Coordinating conjunctions
2. Adverbial conjunctions
3. A stand-alone semicolon (;)

In a compound sentence, the conjunctions or semicolons are placed <u>in the middle</u> between the two independent clauses like so:

IC   **conjunction or semicolon**   IC

Coordinating Conjunctions

One way to join two independent clauses is by using coordinating conjunctions. A **coordinating conjunction** joins clauses that are grammatically equal to show they are similar in importance and structure. It also shows how the clauses are related to each other. The coordinating conjunction comes in the middle between two independent clauses and requires a <u>comma right before</u> the conjunction.

IC, Coordinating Conjunction IC.

I ate cereal, and I drank milk.

Make sure that you do not put the comma after the coordinating conjunction; the sentence is only correct when a coordinating conjunction follows a comma.

Incorrect: **I ate cereal and, I drank milk.**
Correct: **I ate cereal, and I drank milk.**

The meaning of the connection changes depending on which conjunction is used.

I ate cake, and my girlfriend ate cookies.

I ate cake, but my girlfriend ate cookies.

👆 MEMORY TIP

You can remember the seven coordinating conjunctions by using the acronym **FANBOYS,** which is based on the first letter of each coordinating conjunction.

F	**for**	(meaning "because" or "since")
A	**and**	(meaning "in addition")
N	**nor**	(meaning "and neither")
B	**but**	(meaning "on the contrary" or "however")
O	**or**	(meaning "alternatively")
Y	**yet**	(meaning "even," "however," or "but")
S	**so**	(meaning "therefore")

It is only when joining two independent clauses that a coordinating conjunction requires a comma in front of it. Remember that these seven conjunctions can also join two nouns, two verbs, or two prepositional phrases. Do not put commas before these connector words if they are not used as conjunctions or not used to join independent clauses.

I like tea <u>or</u> coffee. (two nouns)
He was angry <u>and</u> tired. (two verbs)
The cat is in the room <u>and</u> on the bed. (two prepositional phrases)

BUILDING SKILLS 6-2: Identifying Coordinating Conjunctions

Read the following sentences and circle the coordinating conjunction (or FANBOYS) being used. Some sentences may not have a conjunction.

Example: She is a dedicated athlete, so she practices for four hours every day.

1. They watched the parade, and they watched the fireworks.
2. They watched the parade and the fireworks.
3. They watched the Fourth of July parade in the blazing sun.
4. They did not watch the parade, nor did they watch the fireworks.
5. The party was a hit, but everyone was tired from dancing.
6. The bus ride was quiet, for everyone was thinking about the trip.
7. She called him twice on his cell phone, yet he never answered.
8. The bus stop is not far from here, so let us keep walking.
9. They went to the zoo to see the new panda bear exhibit.
10. They went to the zoo, and they packed a picnic basket.

BUILDING SKILLS 6-3: Writing with Coordinating Conjunctions

Combine the following sentences using coordinating conjunctions (or FANBOYS).

Example: Matthew wants to relocate to Canada. He wants to be closer to his family.

Matthew wants to relocate to Canada, so he can be closer to his family.

1. Kia threw herself into her studies. Her home life was very difficult.

_____

2. I hate having lunch alone. I try to find someone to eat with me.

_____

3. Jamie is majoring in physics. He hopes to work for NASA.

_____

4. The student council election is this week. I have no idea who is running.

_____

5. On-campus parking can be extremely difficult. The situation will be worse soon. _____
_____

6. I worked as a bank teller. I was bored with that job by the second week.
_____
_____

7. I do not want to derail the lecture. The instructor does not like interruptions or questions. _____
_____

8. I know my weaknesses as a test-taker. I am working to improve them.
_____
_____

9. Relaxation training is a good strategy to overcome test anxiety. It may involve learning how to breathe. _____
_____

10. I feel miserable. My allergies are acting up. I am coming down with a cold.
_____
_____

Adverbial Conjunctions

Another way to produce the compound sentence is by using adverbial conjunctions. Adverbial conjunctions join two independent clauses and, like coordinating conjunctions, give information about the relationship between the two clauses. An adverbial conjunction makes the connection between ideas of clauses clearer and more precise.

> I ate cake, <u>and</u> my girlfriend ate cookies.

Whereas coordinating conjunctions require an initial comma when joining independent clauses, adverbial conjunctions require a semicolon in front and a comma behind.

> I ate cake; <u>similarly</u>, my girlfriend ate banana bread.

Like coordinating conjunctions (or FANBOYS), adverbial conjunctions come in the middle between two independent clauses, but adverbial conjunctions require the use of a semicolon before and a comma after them.

IC; adverbial conjunction, IC.

> I ate cake; <u>however</u>, my girlfriend ate cookies.

Each adverbial conjunction stresses a particular relationship between the two ICs; therefore, consider your choice of conjunction carefully.

; However,	I ate cereal; however, I did not drink milk. (notice the word order)
; Otherwise,	I ate cereal; otherwise, I would have had to drink milk. (notice word order)
; Therefore,	I ate cereal; therefore, I drank milk.
; Similarly,	I ate cereal; similarly, I drank milk.
; Hence,	I ate cereal; hence, I drank milk.
; On the other hand,	I did not eat cereal; on the other hand, I drank milk.
; Thus,	I ate cereal; thus, I drank milk.
; Meanwhile,	I ate cereal; meanwhile, Tom drank milk.
; Additionally,	I ate cereal; additionally, I drank milk.
; Moreover,	I ate cereal; moreover, I drank milk.
; Also,	I ate cereal; also, I drank milk.
; Consequently,	I ate cereal; consequently, I drank milk.
; As a matter of fact,	I ate cereal; as a matter of fact, I drank milk, too.
; Then,	I ate cereal; then, I drank milk.

In addition, there are more adverbial conjunctions like: *nonetheless, nevertheless, furthermore, as a result, besides, instead, indeed, in fact, subsequently, for instance, likewise, accordingly,* and *for example.* Consult the Memory Tip on page 141 for a varied list of adverbial conjunctions.

🖐 MEMORY TIP

You can remember the adverbial conjunctions by using the acronym HOT SHOT MAMA CAT, which is based on the first letter of each adverbial conjunction. Consider this list of frequently used adverbial conjunctions:

H	; However,	(meaning "but")
O	; Otherwise,	(meaning "if not" "or else")
T	; Therefore,	(meaning "for that reason")
S	; Similarly,	(meaning "likewise")
H	; Hence,	(meaning "for that reason")
O	; On the other hand,	(meaning "in contrast")
T	; Thus,	(meaning "so" or "in this way")
M	; Meanwhile,	(meaning "while")
A	; Additionally,	(meaning "also")
M	; Moreover,	(meaning "in addition")
A	; Also,	(meaning "in addition")
C	; Consequently,	(meaning "so")
A	; As a matter of fact,	(meaning "in fact")
T	; Then,	(meaning "next" or "so")

For ease of reference, you can use this shortened acronym, HOT MAMA.

BUILDING SKILLS 6-4: Identifying Adverbial Conjunctions: HOT SHOT MAMA CAT

Underline the adverbial conjunction (or HOT SHOT MAMA CAT) used in each sentence and insert the correct punctuation.

Example: He had to retire from law enforcement; however, he was an honorable police officer.

1. The rainy season has ended therefore the weather is perfect.

2. The monster appeared on the screen hence the girl fainted.

3. The teacher told us to be quiet however we continued to chat.

4. I will finish my work then we will go to the beach.

5. Grammar is difficult to learn on the other hand communicating correctly is important.

6. Finish your work tonight consequently you will not worry about it tomorrow.

7. Boxing is a demanding sport as a matter of fact it requires great athletic skill and self-discipline.

8. Alan checked around the house for the cat meanwhile Sam searched the neighborhood.

9. Henry supported me in bad times moreover he gave me money.

10. We will go to the supermarket then we will meet our sister at the mall.

BUILDING SKILLS 6-5: Writing with Adverbial Conjunctions

Combine the following sentences using adverbial conjunctions (or a HOT SHOT MAMA CAT).

Example: Marcy enrolled in the nursing program. She is interested in finding a job in health care.
Marcy enrolled in the nursing program; moreover, she is interested in finding a job in health care.

1. The Melbournes took a trip to Europe. The trip was very expensive.

_____

_____

2. It was a very hot summer. Mario bought a new air conditioner.

_____

_____

3. We move in tomorrow. The construction on the house is not complete.

_____

_____

4. Most of the wedding cake was eaten. I managed to find a small crumb.

_____

_____

5. The mall closed for the day. Marcy did not find a birthday gift for her friend.

_____

_____

6. The iPod was on sale. I still could not afford to buy it.

_____

_____

7. We canceled our reservation. We had to pay the penalty fee.

_____

_____

8. The student studied diligently. He did well on the final exam.

_____

_____

9. I needed a new computer. I had to a second part-time job.

_____

_____

10. Mickey's has the best chili. I eat there every Monday.

_____

_____

Semicolons

A third way to join two independent clauses or write a compound sentence is by using a semicolon between the two independent clauses (ICs). A semicolon suggests that there is a relationship between the sentences; however, the relationship is not explicitly stated. Semicolons allow for flexibility in writing when the writer does not want to show the specific connection between the two clauses.

I ate cereal. I drank milk.

I ate cereal; I drank milk.

It might seem easiest to use a semicolon to join clauses rather than having to memorize all the other conjunctions, but if you rely heavily on using semicolons in your sentences, your writing will fall into the "choppy" syndrome. To be a good writer, use varied sentences, avoiding the overuse of any one connecting strategy.

BUILDING SKILLS 6-6: Semicolons

Join these sentences using a semicolon.

Example: He suddenly woke up from a deep sleep. The sun was dazzling his half-open eyes.

He suddenly woke up from a deep sleep; the sun was dazzling his half-open eyes.

1. Candace wanted a chocolate milkshake. They did not have any.

_____

_____

2. I called you several times. You never answered.

_____

_____

3. It is dangerous to be outside in this storm. The air temperature is below the freezing point.

_____

_____

4. Martin was anxious to go to the rock concert. He called his three friends.

_____

_____

5. Tom did not make the team. He trained so hard.

_____

_____

6. I baked a cake for the church gathering. I took it with me.

_____

_____

7. They do not like salsa dancing. They do not like ballroom dancing.

_____

_____

8. Dad wanted pancakes. My brother Milo wanted waffles.

_____

_____

9. I will not clean the litter box. I will feed the cat.

_____

_____

10. School started late today. It had snowed during the night.

_____

_____

BUILDING SKILLS TOGETHER 6-1: Compound Sentences in Writing

In small groups, revise the following passage by creating compound sentences to achieve sentence variety. Use the skills you have learned about the three kinds of compound sentences.

(1) Friends can be a basic source of happiness. (2) We have different friends throughout life. (3) The friendships of adolescence and young adulthood are the closest we ever form. (4) They ease the normal break from parents. (5) They transition us from childhood to independence. (6) Many people believed that men and women couldn't become close friends. (7) They believed that men and women couldn't go without getting romantically involved. (8) Over the years, both genders have worked together. (9) They have come to share more interests. (10) The belief that there cannot be male-female friendships has changed. (11) Men and women who become friends benefit from such a relationship. (12) For men, such a friendship offers support and nurturing. (13) Reports show that men like talking and relating to women. (14) They don't get to do that with their male buddies. (15) Women view their friendships with men as casual and lighthearted with less fear of hurt feelings. (16) They especially like getting insight into what men really think of women.

—From Dianne Hales, *An Invitation to Health*

Revised Version: _____

_____

_____

_____

_____

_____
_____
_____
_____
_____
_____
_____
_____
_____
_____
_____
_____
_____
- -

🕯 BUILDING SKILLS TOGETHER 6-2: Compound
▌ Sentences in Writing

In small groups, revise the following passage by creating compound sentences to achieve sentence variety. Use the skills you have learned about the three kinds of compound sentences.

(1) My friend Gloria was a first-semester student at a large college campus. (2) She found college life a bit overwhelming. (3) She was excited about her major of forensic chemistry. (4) The crime shows on television were her favorites. (5) She watched them all each week. (6) She pictured herself as an investigator solving headline cases. (7) Gloria envisioned herself hunched over laboratory equipment, testing for fibers or DNA, and actually breaking criminal cases. (8) Her academic advisor in college recommended she take an "Introduction to Criminology" course. (9) He explained to Gloria how this class would help her understand the field of criminology. (10) It would teach her to understand the criminal mind. (11) Gloria registered for this course. (12) She hoped she would get a good professor. (13) She wanted to connect with someone who had worked in the field.

Revised Version: _____
_____
_____
_____
_____

_____

Joining an Independent Clause with a Dependent Clause: Complex Sentences

A third kind of sentence is the **complex sentence.** This sentence consists of joining independent clauses (IC) and dependent clauses (DC). Remember that a dependent clause has a subject and a verb but does not express a complete thought; it cannot stand on its own as a complete sentence. Dependent clauses need to be joined to independent clauses.

> **MEMORY TIP**
>
> The complex sentence is aptly called complex because the order <u>of the dependent and independent clauses determines how the sentence is punctuated</u>.

Subordinating Conjunctions

Because a dependent clause by its very nature is subordinate or inferior to an independent clause, the only option for connecting clauses in a complex sentence is what is called a **subordinating conjunction.** While coordinating and adverbial conjunctions are effective to use in joining two things of equal importance, subordinating conjunctions can show that one idea is more important than another. Therefore, the idea in the independent clause is more important while the idea in the subordinate or dependent clause (made subordinate or dependent by the subordinating conjunction) is less important. In fact, the **dependent** or **subordinate clause** supplies a time, reason, condition, etc. for the independent clause.

Dependent clause explains why we went home
↓
[After the train left,] we went home. ← _Independent clause_

Subordinating conjunctions are a group of words that connect a dependent clause with an independent clause. They always come at the beginning of a dependent clause. The dependent clause can come either before or after the independent clause.

No comma   Dependent clause
↓   ↓
I ate cereal when I drank milk.

Here, the subordinating conjunction is sandwiched between two clauses; it does not require any punctuation.

Comma   Independent clause
↓   ↓
When I ate cereal, I drank milk.

Here, the dependent clause comes first and cannot stand on its own, so it needs a comma to prepare the reader for the forthcoming independent clause, which will complete its meaning.

MEMORY TIP

For complex sentences, remember that:

- If the subordinating conjunction is <u>between</u> two clauses, <u>no punctuation is required.</u>
- If the subordinating conjunction is <u>at the beginning</u> of the first clause, <u>put a comma to separate</u> the first clause from the second clause.

As with all other conjunctions, subordinating conjunctions indicate subtle shifts in meaning depending on which conjunction is used.

<u>Since my girlfriend ate the cake</u>, I will drink the milk.
<u>Jenny ate the cake before she drank the milk.</u>
<u>Because you don't like cake, we didn't go to the party.</u>

Each subordinating conjunction stresses a particular relationship; therefore, consider your choice of conjunction carefully.

As   *because* or *when*
<u>As</u> she is my friend, I will help her.
We watched <u>as</u> the train left the station.

As if   *in a similar way*
She talks <u>as if</u> she knows everything.

After   *later in time*
<u>After</u> the concert ended, we went home.

As long as   *if* or *while*
As long as we cooperate, we can be released for ransom.
They have lived there as long as I have known them.

As soon as   *immediately when*
Call me as soon as you can.

As though   *in a similar way*
It looks as though there will be a hurricane.

Although or **though**   *in spite of the fact that*
Although it was midnight, we did not feel sleepy.

Before   *earlier than*
I arrived before the restaurant opened.

Because   *for the reason that*
We had to wait because we arrived too early.

If   *on condition that*
If the actor is here, we will see him.

Even if   *in spite of a possibility*
I am going out even if it rains.

Providing or **provided**   *on condition that*
All will be well providing you stay alert.

Since   *as, because*
Since you are here, you can help me.

Unless   *except when, if not*
Unless Mr. Tom helps us, we cannot succeed.

Until or **till**   *up to the time when*
I will wait until I hear from the interviewers.

Whereas   *because* or *on the other hand*
Whereas this is a public exhibit, it is open to everyone.
He is charismatic, whereas you are glamorous.

Whether   *if*
I do not know whether they were invited to the party.

While   *at the time when*   *on the other hand*   *although*
While it was snowing, we watched movies.
He is rich while his parents are poor.
While I am not an expert, I will do my best to help you.

MEMORY TIP

You may want to remember the subordinating conjunctions by using the acronym WASBIT, which stands for the following conjunctions:

W	**W**hen, **W**here, **W**herever, **W**henever, **W**hereas, **W**hether, **W**hile
A	**A**s, **A**s if, **A**s long as, **A**s though, **A**lthough
S	**S**ince, **S**o that
B	**B**efore, **B**ecause
I	**I**f
T	**T**hough

There are many more subordinating conjunctions, but these are the most frequently used ones.

BUILDING SKILLS 6-7: Identifying Subordinating Conjunctions

In the following sentences, circle the subordinating conjunction (or WASBIT) and write *comma needed* or *no comma needed* on the line. If a comma is needed, add where necessary.

Example: Since he graduated last summer⊙he has not found a job. <u>comma needed</u>

1. We liked the movie after we read the reviews. _____

2. Whenever Mrs. Stark asked a question she looked at the ceiling. _____

3. The party was a success because the guests knew each other well. _____

4. When she eats seafood she has an allergic reaction. _____

5. After I took a nap I felt so much better. _____

6. Even if it rains on Sunday the trip will proceed as planned. _____

7. I like to go on road trips since I love to drive. _____

8. As they rounded the bend a large bear appeared. _____

9. While the rabbits are cute they are destroying our backyard. _____

10. Betty goes to the beach whenever she can get away from work. _____

11. They bought a house after they won the lottery. _____

12. My car will not start as long as the battery is dead. _____

13. If he fails his biology class he will lose his scholarship. _____

14. The police are trying to determine whether he is the right murder suspect. _____

15. Marcus will become a doctor whereas his sister will become a teacher. _____

BUILDING SKILLS 6-8: Writing with Subordinating Conjunctions

Combine the following sentences using a subordinating conjunction (or WASBIT). Be sure to use the appropriate punctuation.

Example: Snakes are carnivorous animals. They eat nothing but other animals.
<u>Since snakes are carnivorous animals, they eat nothing but other animals.</u>

1. Sally's mother is a mean woman. She visits her regularly.

_____

_____

2. My toddler son found the saltshaker. He sprinkled salt all over the kitchen floor.

_____

_____

3. Tim is sleeping on his brother's couch. He was kicked out from his home.

_____

_____

4. You should go see the new action movie. It is a remarkable story.

_____

_____

5. John's parents just moved to Texas. They had retired earlier this year.

_____

_____

6. Many people came to see the new paintings. The exhibit was controversial.

_____

_____

7. The transcontinental railroad was built. Its construction was considered one of the greatest American technological feats of the nineteenth century.

_____

_____

8. Some popular toys are discovered by accident. People discover something else in the invention process.

   _____

   _____

9. The Mayans built complex structures. They knew mathematics well.

   _____

   _____

10. People expect floods in low areas. The rainy season begins. They take precautions.

    _____

    _____

◖ BUILDING SKILLS TOGETHER 6-3: Complex Sentences in Writing

In small groups, revise the following passage by creating complex sentences to achieve sentence variety. Use the skills you have learned about subordinating conjunctions (or WASBIT).

(1) A hotel concierge's job is not an easy one. (2) She or he may act as tour guide, travel agent, weather reporter, restaurant reviewer, secretary, and more. (3) The most common guest requests a concierge responds to are making dinner reservations, confirming and reissuing airline tickets, or providing maps and directions to local attractions. (4) Many of the requests a concierge responds to are last minute. (5) Being able to handle pressure is an important quality.

(6) Details of how the job of concierge came into being are sketchy. (7) Many believe the profession dates back to the Middle Ages. (8) The doorkeeper of the castle was also keeper of the keys for locking the royal family and guests safely in for the night. (9) In the mid-1970s, several San Francisco hotels brought the concierge concept to America. (10) The concierge would leave messages on guests' pillows informing them of various services. (11) Today, computers facilitate many of the requests. (12) Personal service is the hallmark of the profession.

(13) Most major hotels today have at least one concierge on staff. (14) Every guest request is different or has the potential to be unique. (15) Training as a concierge is not clear-cut. (16) The professional trade organization, The Golden Keys, does set standards. (17) The standards include a

five-year minimum experience in the hotel industry and letters of recommendation from hotel management staff.

—From Chon/Maier, *Welcome to Hospitality: An Introduction*

Revised Version: _____

_____
_____
_____
_____
_____
_____
_____
_____
_____
_____
_____
_____
_____
_____
_____
_____
_____
_____
_____
_____
_____
_____
_____
_____
_____

Joining Multiple Independent and Dependent Clauses: Compound-Complex Sentences

A fourth and final kind of sentence is the **compound-complex sentence**, which consists of two or more independent clauses and one or more dependent clauses.

My father encouraged me to pick up a hobby, <u>so</u> I started collecting stamps; I became rich <u>when</u> I started a company that acquires <u>and</u> sells rare stamps; consequently, my hobby is now my livelihood.

This sentence is really five clauses combined together through the use of conjunctions and a semicolon. Here is what the simple sentences look like:

My father encouraged me to pick up a hobby.

I started collecting stamps.

I became rich.

I started a company trading rare stamps.

My hobby is now my livelihood.

Notice how all four connecting strategies are used: a coordinating conjunction, a subordinating conjunction, a semicolon, and an adverbial conjunction. You are at liberty to use all these tools in adding variety to your sentence structure.

BUILDING SKILLS 6-9: Compound-Complex Sentences

Using a variety of conjunctions and/or semicolons, combine the following simple sentences into compound-complex sentences.

Example: The blue whale can produce sounds up to 188 decibels.

This is the loudest sound produced by a living animal.

This sound can be detected as far away as 500 miles.

Because the blue whale can produce sounds up to 188 decibels, it is the loudest sound produced by a living animal; in fact, this sound can be detected as far away as 500 miles.

1. The monster appeared on screen.
   The child fainted.
   The audience gasped.

   _____

   _____

   _____

2. He plays the drums.
   He turns the volume up.
   The neighbors complain.

   _____

   _____

   _____

3. Amos went to the rap concert.
   He did not enjoy himself.
   His seat was in the back lower deck.

   _____

   _____

   _____

4. I will do the dishes.
   You will vacuum the house.
   We can go to the mall._____

   _____

   _____

👆 MEMORY TIP

Kinds of Sentences

1. **Simple Sentence = 1 Independent Clause**

   I drink milk.
   I eat cereal.

2. **Compound Sentence = 2 Independent Clauses**

   • Coordinating Conjunctions: FANBOYS

for, and, nor, but, or, yet, so

   I drink milk, and I eat cereal.
   I drink milk, so I eat cereal.

   • Adverbial Conjunctions: HOT SHOT MAMA CAT
   I drink milk; therefore, I eat cereal.
   I drink milk; then, I eat cereal.

; also,	; therefore,	; otherwise,	; consequently,
; besides,	; nonetheless,	; furthermore,	; nevertheless,
; instead,	; however,	; for instance,	; accordingly,
; indeed,	; moreover,	; likewise,	; for example,
; in fact,	; as a result,	; in addition,	; meanwhile,
; thus,	; then,	; similarly,	; hence,
; in fact,	; subsequently,	; on the other hand,	

   • Semicolon: **;**
   I drink milk**;** I eat cereal.

3. **Complex Sentence = 1 Independent Clause and 1 Dependent Clause**

   Subordinating Conjunctions: WASBIT
   • IC + WASBIT + IC = no comma needed
   I drink milk when I eat cereal.

   • WASBIT+ DC, IC = Comma needed in the middle
   When I drink milk, I eat cereal.

When, where, wherever, whenever, whereas, whether, while, as, as if, as long as, as though, although, after, so that, since, before, because, behind, if, in order, though, until, unless, rather than, provided that

4. **Compound-Complex Sentence = 2 or more Independent Clauses with 2 or more Dependent Clauses**

   Use a mix of FANBOYS, HOT SHOT MAMA CAT, WASBIT, and semicolon to join.

❚ BUILDING SKILLS TOGETHER 6-4: Writing Different ❚ Kinds of Sentences

Working with a partner, complete the following sentences based on the topic provided. The sentences have been started for you.

Topic: Sara and her dream house

Simple Sentences:

1. The neighborhood _____

2. The house _____

Compound Sentence: Using coordinating conjunctions (or FANBOYS)

3. It was the house of her dreams _____
_____

4. She contacted her real estate agent _____
_____

Compound Sentence: Using adverbial conjunctions (or HOT SHOT MAMA CAT)

5. The price for the house was expensive _____
_____

6. She was ready to negotiate _____
_____

Complex Sentence: Using subordinating conjunctions (or WASBIT)

7. Although she made a good offer _____
_____

8. The sellers were not easy to work with _____
_____

Compound-Complex Sentence: using 2 or more conjunctions

9. She bought the house _____
_____
_____

10 After she moved into the house _____
_____
_____

◍ BUILDING SKILLS TOGETHER 6-5: Writing Sentences and Paragraphs

In small groups, create a paragraph of 5 to 7 sentences using the answers to the corresponding questions below. Rotate turns, so each member in the group has a chance to create a sentence. Once you have completed your answers, rewrite the sentences into a correctly punctuated paragraph and share your text with the class. Your paragraph may have a tragic or funny tone and should be imagined, not drawn from real-life events.

Sentence one:	Simple sentence ᵏ
Question one:	Our trip to _____ was memorable.

Sentence two:	Compound sentence using a coordinating conjunction (or FANBOYS)
Question two:	When did you go on the trip and who was with you?

Sentence three:	Complex sentence using a subordinating conjunction (or WASBIT)
Question three:	How far did you have to travel to get to your destination?

Sentence four:	Compound sentence using an adverbial conjunction (or a HOT SHOT MAMA CAT)
Question four:	Why did you go on that trip?

Sentence five:	Compound sentence using a coordinating conjunction (or FANBOYS)
Question five:	What were some things you did on the trip?

Sentence six:	Complex sentence using a subordinating conjunction (or WASBIT)
Question six:	Did you like what you did on the trip? Why or why not?

➥

Sentence seven: Simple sentence

Question seven: Would you recommend that trip to others?

◖ BUILDING SKILLS TOGETHER 6-6: Improving Essays with Varied Kinds of Sentences

In small groups, revise the following essay to achieve sentence variety. Use the skills you have learned about conjunctions and about compound, complex, and compound-complex sentence structures.

(1) A major problem in health care today is determining what drug and what dosage should be used for a patient. (2) Individuals react to medications in different ways. (3) Some individuals need large amounts of pain medication. (4) Others need smaller quantities. (5) A blood pressure medication works well for one individual. (6) It is not effective for another patient. (7) An antibiotic cures an infection in one person. (8) It causes an allergic reaction that kills another person. (9) Pharmacogenetics is the science of prescribing medicine based on a person's unique genetic makeup. (10) It is the start of a revolution in personalizing treatment for a particular individual.

(11) Researchers are using genetic information about individuals to try to determine their reactions to different medications. (12) Scientists have proved that there is a gene in a person's body that controls how a drug is absorbed, used, and eliminated. (13) This gene may be different from person to person. (14) By learning an individual's genetic makeup, a physician could prescribe the exact medication and dosage that would be most beneficial to a patient.

(15) Imagine a future where people will have a computer chip that contains all of their genetic information. (16) This information will be scanned before medication is given to a patient. (17) A computer will analyze the information and determine the patient's compatibility with the medication. (18) The exact dosage needed by the patient will be revealed.

(19) This process raises concerns about patient confidentiality, privacy, and legal regulations. (20) It has the potential to save lives. (21) A medicine given to

a patient should be based on the person's specific needs. (22) Diseases will be treated correctly and eventually cured.

—From Louise Simmers, *Introduction to Health Science Technology*

Revised Version: _____

_____

_____

_____

_____

_____

_____

_____

_____

_____

_____

_____

_____

_____

_____

_____

_____

_____

_____

_____

_____

_____

_____

_____

_____

CHAPTER SIX SKILLS REVIEW 1: Kinds of Sentences

Determine what type of sentence is being used. Write simple (S), compound (CP), complex (CX), or compound-complex (CPCX) on the line.

_____ 1. She admired the ocean view as she sat there lost in thought.

_____ 2. We must stay here because she has left with our only means of transportation.

_____ 3. The weather was bad; they could not visit their ailing grandmother.

_____ 4. Summer was coming to an end, so they had to go home; however, they promised their friends they would visit again next summer.

_____ 5. Although Ben would like to do more acting, Mason is more interested in football.

_____ 6. Mitch and Sara have planned a graduation party for Maddy.

_____ 7. Sam called twice today, but he could not reach Tim.

_____ 8. The wind was cold; however, I did not have a coat.

_____ 9. Mr. Goodman is very knowledgeable about anthropology, but he is strict in class.

_____ 10. If you walk quickly, you can catch the last morning bus.

_____ 11. If you finish your work tonight, you will not have to worry about it tomorrow.

_____ 12. Wrestling is a demanding sport; in fact, it requires strong self-discipline and great physical fitness.

_____ 13. It is difficult to learn all the grammar rules, but grammar skills are essential for success in college writing.

_____ 14. While the summer is pleasant, I prefer the fall season.

_____ 15. The rescue helicopter landed on top of the mountain.

_____ 16. I saw that awful movie when I was in high school.

_____ 17. The winding road up the hill was closed; we had to turn around.

_____ 18. School started late today since it snowed last night.

_____ 19. When she eats seafood, she has an allergic reaction; therefore, she avoids going to seafood restaurants.

_____ 20. Although the rabbits are cute, they are destroying our vegetable garden.

CHAPTER SIX SKILLS REVIEW 2: Sentence Combining

Combine the following pairs of sentences using any of the three kinds of conjunctions—coordinating, adverbial, or subordinating (FANBOYS, HOT SHOT MAMA CAT, or WASBIT)—or the semicolon. Please write out the whole sentence.

1. The suspected criminal ran into the street.
   The police officers chased him.

   _____

   _____

   _____

2. Students need to enjoy their college years.
   It is important to study well.

   _____

   _____

   _____

3. We will move in tomorrow.
   The construction on the house is not complete.

   _____

   _____

   _____

4. I bought a new smartphone.
   It is too complicated for me.

   _____

   _____

   _____

5. Larry likes to work with numbers.
   He is studying finance.

   _____

   _____

   _____

6. My brother is a single parent.
   He needs a job with a flexible schedule.

   _____

   _____

   _____

7. I studied my chemistry notes for an hour.
   I fell asleep on the sofa.

   _____

   _____

   _____

8. Ben has a terrible cold.
   He insists on coming to work.

   _____

   _____

   _____

9. My mother opened the letter from the lawyers.
   She screamed with joy.

   _____

   _____

   _____

10. Jeans with brand names are expensive.
    I buy my jeans from a thrift store.

    _____

    _____

    _____

11. The wind howled ferociously.
    My candle flickered and blew out.
    The door and windows rattled loudly.
    I saw the ghost.

    _____

    _____

    _____

12. Alex likes Annabel.
    Annabel loves Jason.

    _____

    _____

    _____

13. Helen wants to vacation in Spain.
    She lost all her money on a bad business investment.
    Spain will remain her dream destination.

    _____

    _____

    _____

14. I want to download music for my iPod.
I cannot find the songs I like on iTunes.

_____

_____

_____

15. Many Americans cannot afford to have health insurance.
They see doctors only in emergencies.

_____

_____

_____

CHAPTER SEVEN: The Seventh Building Block
Avoiding Common Sentence Errors

In previous chapters, you learned about subjects and verbs and how they can be combined with conjunctions to create different kinds of sentences. Writers who understand the value of adding variety and interest to their sentences will make some errors as they experiment; these errors often fall into three familiar patterns that have been given specific names: **fragments**, **run-ons**, and **comma splices**. This chapter explains these common sentence errors and provides simple solutions for fixing them.

FRAGMENTS

You know that a complete sentence must contain both a subject and verb. A **fragment** is an incomplete sentence that does not make sense and cannot stand on its own. A fragment has one of the following five problems:

1. **Sentence is missing a subject.**

   Cannot be my friend. (fragment)

   Who cannot be my friend? This sentence does not have a subject. To fix the fragment, add a subject, so it becomes a complete sentence.

   <u>Tom</u> **cannot be my friend.** (complete)

   Remember that a subject can be a person, place, thing, or idea.

   Does not have to lead bitter fights. (fragment)
   <u>Expressing a political opinion</u> **does not have to lead to bitter fights.** (complete)

A subject can also be a pronoun.

> <u>This</u> does not have to lead to bitter fights. (complete)

2. **Sentence is missing a verb.**

> The girl in the red hood. (fragment)

What is the girl in the red hood doing? We don't know; there is no verb. To fix the fragment, add a verb, so it becomes a complete sentence.

> The girl with the red hood <u>walked</u> toward me. (complete)

Remember that a verb can be a state of being as well as an action.

> Unselfish love toward another human being. (fragment)
> Unselfish love toward another human being is <u>rare</u>. (complete)

3. **Sentence is missing both a subject and a verb.**

> At the end of the day.

Prepositional phrases like this may seem like complete thoughts, but they are not.

> On the soccer field. (fragment)
> After a long silence. (fragment)
> To play the piano. (fragment)

To fix the fragment, add an **independent clause** (which by definition contains both a subject and a verb) to the phrase.

> At the end of the day, <u>Gina watches the sun set</u>. (complete)
> <u>The players cheered</u> on the soccer field. (complete)
> <u>I am longing</u> to play the piano. (complete)

4. **Sentence is missing a helping verb.** The sentence has an _–ing_ verb with no helping verb such as _is, are, was, w_

> Barry running to the door. (fragmen

To fix the fragment, add a helping ver

> Barry <u>was</u> running to the door. (com

5. **Sentence is a dependent clause that c** contains both a subject and a verb, a a complete thought and should not be were a sentence.

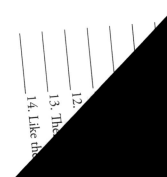

When the band started to play. (fragment)
While she talked on the phone. (fragment)
That Jerry described. (fragment)

To fix the fragment, add an independent clause.

When the band started to play, <u>people got up to dance.</u> (complete)
<u>Jerry interrupted her</u> while she talked on the phone. (complete)
<u>She couldn't understand the directions</u> that Jerry described. (complete)

> **MEMORY TIP**
>
> A fragment is not a sentence because it:
> - Does not make sense on its own.
> - Needs information added to it to make it complete.

BUILDING SKILLS 7-1: Identifying Fragments

Determine if each phrase is correct or fragmented. Write *S* for sentence and *F* for fragment.

Example: <u>F</u> Walking down the long path to the house.

_____ 1. Bill's sick mother.

_____ 2. Mr. Smith teaches history at a community college in California.

_____ 3. Behind the television and under the shelf.

_____ 4. Lauren and Ryan's ninth wedding anniversary.

_____ 5. Most of the animals starved during the severe drought.

_____ 6. Nicole wishing she had a good role in the Shakespeare play.

_____ 7. Swims across the pool in a hurry.

_____ 8. While I make the fruit salad for the party.

_____ 9. At ninety-six, Grandma is old.

_____ 10. I need a cup of coffee to wake up.

_____ 11. The boy in the orange bathing suit.

The plane flashing its take off lights.

lma my best friend from school.

e one at Matt's house.

_____ 15. He looks very happy today.

_____ 16. Running through the sprinklers during the hottest part of the day.

_____ 17. After you wash the dirty dishes.

_____ 18. Especially the clothes I wear.

_____ 19. When the rain ended this morning.

_____ 20. The noisy students talking in class.

_____ 21. The brown dog with the fleas on his back.

_____ 22. Suddenly stopping in traffic.

_____ 23. Which is a difficult situation.

_____ 24. The old pickup truck refusing to start.

_____ 25. Harry and Larry at the company luncheon.

_____ 26. Since the heater broke.

_____ 27. On the right of the table with the flower vase on it.

_____ 28. The book on the floor in the bedroom.

_____ 29. Have been through so much.

_____ 30. It is a beautiful warm day.

BUILDING SKILLS 7-2: Identifying Fragments

Read each sentence and identify what is missing in each fragment. Rewrite the fragments into complete sentences. More than one answer is possible for some sentences.

Missing: Subject
           Verb
           Subject and verb
           Helping verb
           Independent clause

Example: Graduating in 2014. Missing: <u>subject and verb</u>
           <u>Tom will graduate in 2014.</u>

1. The hungry wolves attacking the helpless deer. Missing: _____

   _____

   _____

2. While the graduation party continued. Missing: _____

   _____

   _____

➥

3. The dinner from the Mexican restaurant. Missing: _____

   _____

   _____

4. Barry's tweed coat. Missing: _____

5. The eccentric woman painting her orange house. Missing:_____

   _____

   _____

6. Pouring hot chocolate fudge on the cake. Missing: _____

   _____

   _____

7. After the summer ends. Missing: _____

   _____

   _____

8. On the granite kitchen counter by the cooktop. Missing: _____

   _____

   _____

9. And spent the afternoon working on the marketing project. Missing:_____

   _____

   _____

10. Because I took the advice of a dear friend. Missing: _____

    _____

    _____

🕯️ BUILDING SKILLS TOGETHER 7-1: Correcting Fragments in Writing

Work in small groups to determine if there are fragments in this passage. Write *F* for fragment or *S* for sentence next to the corresponding numbers and then revise the paragraph to correct the faulty sentences.

(1) Summer is supposed to be a pleasant time. (2) Going to the mountains or beach. (3) Surfing, camping, and other fun activities. (4) Even just strolling in the early evening hours. (5) Unfortunately, not everyone can enjoy the season. (6) For some people, summer being pure agony.

(7) For instance, my grandmother who has heart disease. (8) Suffers terribly in the heat. (9) Because her heart cannot pump fast enough to circulate

her blood and to disperse her body's heat. (10) Her blood pressure spikes. (11) Feeling ill. (12) The solution is for her to stay in her air-conditioned house for the whole summer. (13) Gets rather dull.

(14) Infants and toddlers playing all the time in the heat. (15) Because their bodies have not yet developed the ability to dispel heat. (16) The hot temperatures bothering them. (17) Parents are frustrated because they cannot entertain their young ones indoors or force them to slow down.

(18) People who reside in apartments cannot enjoy the summer either. (19) Many apartments not having cross-ventilation. (20) So the hot air settling in the small, stuffy rooms. (21) Also, apartment residents having no backyards. (22) Having no outdoor place to enjoy a mild summer day.

1. _____	12. _____
2. _____	13. _____
3. _____	14. _____
4. _____	15. _____
5. _____	16. _____
6. _____	17. _____
7. _____	18. _____
8. _____	19. _____
9. _____	20. _____
10. _____	21. _____
11. _____	22. _____

RUN-ONS

Run-ons (RO), also called run-together sentences, are sentence errors made up of two side-by-side independent clauses (ICs) that have no punctuation between them. The lack of punctuation makes it difficult for a reader to follow the movement from one complete thought to the other.

We did not hear about the party until Friday we had to change our plans.

Even if a conjunction is added between two independent clauses, punctuation must be added to create a big enough pause for the reader's brain to understand the sentence correctly.

We did not hear about the party until Friday, <u>so</u> we had to change our plans.

> **MEMORY TIP**
>
> Run-ons are sentence errors that look do not include the correct punctuation and look like this:
>
> Independent Clause Independent Clause

To fix run-ons, use one of the following solutions:

1. Add a <u>period</u> between the two independent clauses.

   We did not hear about the party until Friday. We had to change our plans.

2. Add a <u>semicolon</u> between the two independent clauses.

   We had to change our plans; we did not hear about the party until Friday.

3. Add a <u>conjunction and punctuate</u> correctly:
   a. , + coordinating conjunction (FANBOYS).

   We did not hear about the party until Friday, so we had to change our plans.

   b. ; + adverbial conjunction + , (HOT SHOT MAMA CAT).

   We did not hear of the party until Friday; therefore, we changed our plans.

   c. subordinating conjunction (WASBIT) with or without comma.

   When we heard about the party, we changed our plans.
   We changed our plans when we heard about the party.

BUILDING SKILLS 7-3: Identifying Run-ons

Read each sentence and if it is a run-on sentence write *RO*, and if it is correct, write *S* for sentence.

Example: <u>RO</u> The longest living cells in the body are brain cells they can live an entire lifetime.

_____ 1. The mother listened to her son she knew something bad had happened.

_____ 2. My job has been boring; not many customers come in to buy.

_____ 3. The gourmet ice cream store is closed for it lost a lot of money.

_____ 4. The back roads are covered with snow it is dangerous to drive.

_____ 5. Anna's new boss is nice since he gave her the day off.

_____ 6. Jess cooked the steak dinner Tina washed the dishes.

_____ 7. We covered all the furniture before we started painting inside.

_____ 8. I cannot trust Manny and Marie they gossip about others all the time.

_____ 9. Our neighbors just moved from Florida and they seem friendly.

_____ 10. The concert lasted for four hours the musicians were exhausted.

_____ 11. The thunderstorm ended quickly; the damage was astounding.

_____ 12. Candace missed her flight so she had to take a later one.

_____ 13. The microwave is on sale I still cannot afford to buy it.

_____ 14. The waffles smell delicious, and I will have some.

_____ 15. The baby finally drifted to sleep she had been crying for hours.

_____ 16. Randy left his sweatshirt in the sun so it faded.

_____ 17. Mom wanted to make spaghetti, but she did not have the ingredients.

_____ 18. Lasagna is my favorite food however I eat it only once a month.

_____ 19. One mouse ran into the pantry the other mouse ran under the kitchen table.

_____ 20. We could go to the beach, or we could stay home.

COMMA SPLICES

Comma splice errors, like run-ons, occur when two independent clauses are placed side by side. If a comma is chosen as the punctuation mark between the two sentences, an error occurs: the comma "splices" or attempts to join the ideas, but, in fact, a stronger pause is needed between two independent clauses. This error can be compared to a driver who puts his foot on the brake at a stop sign, but does not come to a complete stop. That is illegal in traffic, and it is incorrect in grammar. A full "stop" must be created in one of three ways:

1. Take out the comma and add a <u>period</u> between the two ICs.
   I ate cereal. I drank milk.
2. Change the comma to a <u>semicolon</u> between the two ICs.
   I ate cereal; I drank milk.

3. Add a <u>conjunction and punctuate</u> it correctly:
   a. , + coordinating conjunction (FANBOYS)
      I ate cereal, and I drank milk.
   b. ; + adverbial conjunction (HOT SHOT MAMA CAT)
      I ate cereal; consequently, I drank milk.
   c. subordinating conjunction with or without a comma (WASBIT)
      I ate cereal when I drank milk.
                    OR
      When I ate cereal, I drank milk.

 MEMORY TIP

A **comma splice** is an error that looks like this:

Independent Clause, Independent Clause

BUILDING SKILLS 7-4: Identifying Comma Splices

Read each sentence and if the sentence is a comma splice, write *CS*. If it is correct, write *S* for sentence.

Example: <u>CS</u> The Great Wall of China is more than 2,000 years old, it remains one of the great wonders of the world.

_____ 1. I am a poor man, I am happy.

_____ 2. If I were a poor man, I think I would be happy.

_____ 3. Coffee may be harmful, it tastes good especially in the morning.

_____ 4. The sun was shining; the birds were singing.

_____ 5. When a room is cold, it is impossible to work.

_____ 6. We have changed our project topic, we have to start all over.

_____ 7. I would like to go to the picnic, but I have to work today.

_____ 8. I will scream if you open your mouth to talk.

_____ 9. A few clouds rolled in and, we felt depressed.

_____ 10. I collect autographs consequently, I go to a lot of movie premieres.

_____ 11. The fire alarm rang, we grabbed our things and ran out the door.

_____ 12. The managers flew to the convention, but the employees drove to it.

_____ 13. You have been told to refrain from talking in class, this time you have to bear the consequences of your actions.

_____ 14. Final exams should be eliminated, they just pull down a student's grade.

_____ 15. The teams took to the field, but the referees had forgotten to bring a ball.

_____ 16. I prefer fancy restaurants but, I like fast-food places too.

_____ 17. I have always liked reading about current events, I like to know where the world is heading.

_____ 18. Strawberry milk is nutritious however, unflavored milk has fewer calories.

_____ 19. It is important to use correct grammar, for that enables your reader to understand your message.

_____ 20. His love of animals is great, he plans on becoming a veterinarian.

BUILDING SKILLS 7-5: Correcting Run-ons and Comma Splices

Identify the following sentence errors and write *RO* or *CS* on the line. Then rewrite the sentences to correct them.

Example: RO The name *Japan* means land of the rising sun and the red circle on the Japanese flag is a rising sun.
The name *Japan* means land of the rising sun, and the red circle on the Japanese flag is a rising sun.

_____ 1. He completed the new task his boss gave him a raise.

_____ 2. We canceled the beach trip, the weather was bad.

_____ 3. Greg is an expert skier he won two trophies.

_____ 4. The editor approved the book proposal, the writer could begin writing.

_____ 5. The fire burned for ten minutes yet it caused a lot of damage.

BUILDING SKILLS TOGETHER 7-2: Correcting Run-ons and Comma Splices in Writing

Work in small groups to determine if there are runs-ons and comma splices in this essay. Write *RO, CS,* or *S* next to the corresponding numbers and then revise the paragraph to correct the faulty sentences.

(1) Many people are depressed on their birthdays. (2) Birthdays are terrible days, I think they should be eliminated. (3) If you are one who enjoys birthdays you probably haven't even considered the problem. (4) There are several reasons for disliking birthdays.

(5) The classic reason is that a birthday reminds us that we are getting older. (6) While that is true it is better than the alternative. (7) The first one is departing this world although most people are not eager to do so. (8) The second alternative is eternal youth like what Peter Pan and his gang of boys preferred, we all know what happened to them in the end. (9) I for one would not want to spend eighty years as a two-year-old.

(10) Another reason for birthday depression is that we are afraid no one will remember, that the day will pass as just a regular day. (11) That would be depressing, it is disheartening. (12) It proves that nobody cares it shows us that we are not important to anybody. (13) We feel the world is completely oblivious to our existence it does not even know that we are alive. (14) All our friends who admit to liking us are simply frauds. (15) They not only neglect to wish us "Happy Birthday" but they also fail to give us the time of day.

(16) There is a cure for birthday depression let us get rid of birthdays!

1. _____	9. _____
2. _____	10. _____
3. _____	11. _____
4. _____	12. _____
5. _____	13. _____
6. _____	14. _____
7. _____	15. _____
8. _____	16. _____

MEMORY TIP

Avoid the common sentence errors of fragments, run-ons, and comma splices by writing these kinds of sentences: simple, compound, complex, or compound-complex.

Remember to use the appropriate punctuation for each type of sentence. Refer to Chapter Six or Appendix A for complete details on the four types of sentences.

BUILDING SKILLS TOGETHER 7-3: Correcting Faulty Sentences

Work in small groups. For each sentence, write *F*, *CS*, *RO*, or *S* for the sentence next to the corresponding number. Then, rewrite the paragraph to correct the problems you have recognized.

(1) Marissa is an energetic talker, her listening skills are underdeveloped. (2) She calls herself an attentive friend the truth is that she never really listens to anyone. (3) Marissa is always thinking about what to say next, she only pretends to be listening. (4) Knowing she does not listen to them. (5) Her friends do not discuss important things with her. (6) Tom learned the hard way he told Marissa that his mother had a deadly disease. (7) Marissa was unconcerned and inattentive, she said, "I'm happy to know that." (8) Talking about the dance non-stop. (9) Tom was surprised by Marissa's reaction and he was hurt that she had not been listening to him at all. (10) Tom realized that Marissa thinks she is a loyal friend, she does not realize the truth. (11) She is not a real friend at all her only friend is herself.

1. _____   7. _____

2. _____   8. _____

3. _____   9. _____

4. _____   10. _____

5. _____   11. _____

6. _____

♦ BUILDING SKILLS TOGETHER 7-4: Combining Sentences to Correct Faulty Sentences

With a partner, rewrite this excerpt to correct for faulty sentences.

(1) Nora's turn came, I heard the sound of something slamming then her voice as if butter wouldn't melt in her mouth and another slam and she came out. (2) Her eyes were lowered her head was bowed her hands were joined very low down on her stomach and she walked up the aisle to the side altar looking like a saint. (3) You never saw such an exhibition of devotion, I remembered the devilish malice with which she had tormented me all the way from our door and I wondered were all religious people like that. (4) It was my turn now. (5) With the fear of damnation in my soul. (6) I went in, the confessional door closed of itself behind me.

(7) It was pitch dark, I couldn't see the priest or anything else. (8) Then, beginning to be frightened. (9) In the darkness. (10) It was a matter between God and me and He had all the odds. (11) He knew what my intentions were before I even started I had no chance. (12) All I had ever been told about confession got mixed up in my mind and I knelt to one wall and said: "Bless me, father, for I have sinned; this is my first confession." (13) I waited for a few minutes but nothing happened I tried it on the other wall. (14) Nothing there either he had me spotted all right.

—From Frank O'Connor, "First Confession"

CHAPTER SEVEN SKILLS REVIEW: Common Sentence Errors

Read the following sentences and determine if they are a:

Fragment: F

Run-on: RO

Comma Splice: CS

Sentence: S

_____ 1. Talking on the phone for three hours.

_____ 2. It snowed all night the highways were closed.

_____ 3. Henry's car key left behind on the counter.

_____ 4. Mike is an excellent student, he studies every day.

_____ 5. Jerry running to catch the ball.

_____ 6. Over the dead body in the dirt.

_____ 7. Janie is taking night classes and I am taking morning classes.

_____ 8. Seasons change.

_____ 9. We made plans for the weekend yet, we did not know that Mario would have to work.

_____ 10. Because my car needed an oil change, I took it to the mechanic shop.

_____ 11. Actors waited in line.

_____ 12. My aunt needs to lose weight she is exercising every day.

_____ 13. Tom's interview went well; he thinks he will get the job.

_____ 14. Dr. Rickets postponed the test, everyone in the class was relieved.

_____ 15. I noticed everyone at the party; however I forgot everyone's name.

_____ 16. Moving into my own house was an important event in my life, I gained my freedom.

_____ 17. Cathy is working the day shift and Marco is working the night shift.

_____ 18. Jason works in the garden and his children help him.

_____ 19. Tara partied all weekend, she failed her math test on Monday.

_____ 20. Television is entertaining nevertheless, it is very distracting.

UNIT FOUR: Descriptors, Modifiers, and Parallelism

CHAPTER EIGHT: The Eighth Building Block
Adjectives and Adverbs as Modifiers

Up to this point, you have been learning about how the basic parts of a sentence can be composed and arranged to ensure your writing is not confusing or boring. Now that you have begun to master the tools of sentence clarity and sentence variety, it is time to look at sentence *specificity* and *vitality*.

If you want to tell your friend about a new singer you have become a fan of, you will want to say more than just, "She sings jazz and pop, and she has cut three records." That sentence will not communicate to your friend what makes this singer so special. You may say, however, something like, "She hits an astonishing range of notes on her latest jazz album, and her angrily soulful lyrics send shivers down my spine." Adding descriptive details like these to your sentences requires the use of your seventh building block: **adjectives** and **adverbs**. Adjectives and adverbs are words that modify (identify or describe) other elements in sentences and help you write lively and engaging sentences.

DESCRIPTIVE MODIFIERS

Adjectives add specific details to modify or describe the noun or subject in the sentence, whereas **adverbs** add descriptive details to the verb, adjective, and adverb in the sentence. When these details are added to a sentence, the fundamental building blocks of subjects and verbs stay the same; however, description is used to add specificity to the meaning of the sentence.

The man walked.

You understand what this sentence is about generally; however, you do not know exactly which man or how or where he walked. When you add specific details to this sentence, you get a better description and a more interesting sentence like this:

The <u>tired old</u> man walked <u>slowly and steadily up the street</u>.

The adjectives and adverbs in the above sentence added specificity to the elements and modified the sentence, so you know now which man walked and how he walked.

Adjectives

An **adjective** is a word or words that modify or describe nouns (people, places, things) or pronouns (words that replace nouns). Often, adjectives fall before the noun, and they add information that explains how many, which one, what kind of noun, or whose noun.

 MEMORY TIP

To spot adjectives in a sentence, you must identify the noun first.
Then, ask the following questions about the noun:

    What kind?

    Which one?

    How many?

    Whose?

Consider these examples:
What kind?

The <u>tall</u> girl has a <u>green</u> coat on.
She has <u>short</u> <u>red</u> hair.
She is an <u>English</u> teacher.

Which one?

<u>This</u> month is short.
<u>Next</u> week is a busy one.
The <u>football</u> team is devastated.
The <u>beautiful</u> girl walks home.

How many?

<u>Three</u> boys walked to the bus station.
<u>Several</u> days have passed since the interview.
<u>Five</u> eggs hatched today.
<u>One</u> objective is in mind for the festival.

Whose?

Here is <u>John's</u> suitcase.

He handed me the <u>Smiths'</u> tickets.

👆 **MEMORY TIP**

If you have two or more adjectives that modify the same word, put a comma between them only if the word *and* inserted between the words sounds natural.

He was a bashful dopey person.

Can you add an *and* to the sentence?

He was a bashful <u>and</u> dopey person.

Correct: **He was a bashful, dopey person.**

To locate adjectives, first identify the nouns.

Sue drives an old, small, blue car.

The nouns in this sentence are *Sue* and *car*. No descriptive words are before *Sue*, but a few words are in front of the noun *car*. When you ask the questions: Which one or what kind of car does Sue drive? The answers—old, small, blue— would be the adjectives that describe the noun *car*.

👆 **MEMORY TIP**

The words *this, that, these,* and *those* are adjectives if they come right before a noun.

Pick up these books.

What kind of books? *These books.*

When two or more adjectives are present before a noun, commas are often used to separate them, making it easier for the reader to understand each adjective.

BUILDING SKILLS 8-1: Adding Adjectives

Add adjectives to the following nouns.

Example: An <u>aggressive</u> detective interrogated the suspect.

1. The _____ baby cried all night.

2. An _____ woman walked into the boardroom.

3. The _____ inspector questioned the suspect.

4. The _____ house has been abandoned for a while.

5. A _____ building rose majestically into the sky.

6. The _____ classroom felt stuffy.

7. A _____ swimmer practices for hours.

8. The _____ book lay on the coffee table.

9. This _____ table has seen better days.

10. The _____ idea captivated the audience.

BUILDING SKILLS 8-2: Identifying Adjectives

Underline the adjectives in each sentence.

Example: The <u>old</u> house is a <u>fine</u> example of <u>Victorian</u> architecture.

1. The scratchy loud noise got on my tense nerves.

2. Every day Mary buys fresh green vegetables from the small grocery store.

3. Ron, the handsome and smart man, solved the long math problem.

4. The favorite American team won the last football game.

5. Gray stormy clouds poured cold rain on the sleepy city.

6. Leo bought a big, brown, aggressive dog.

7. Sheila is an unhappy woman because of her three failed marriages.

8. People from all over adored his striking face and engaging personality.

9. The squeaky green door opened for the old man.

10. The tall magnolia trees at the end of the yard have yellow leaves.

Adverbs

An **adverb** is a word that modifies verbs, adjectives, or adverbs. Unlike adjectives, which often fall right before a noun, adverbs fall anywhere in the sentence, even before a verb.

> They <u>usually</u> walk in the evenings.
> He <u>often</u> has cold pizza.

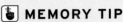 **MEMORY TIP**

To spot adverbs, identify the verb(s) in the sentence and then answer the following questions:

How?

Where?

When?

To what extent—how often or how much?

In identifying adverbs, the questions can be used as in the following examples:

He is talking <u>slowly</u>. (How is he talking?)

The girls went <u>to school</u>. (Where did the girls go?)

The family departed <u>yesterday</u>. (When did the family depart?)

She cooks <u>daily</u>. (How often does she cook?)

I am <u>totally</u> confused. (How much am I confused?)

It is <u>too</u> cold! (How is it?)

Many adverbs are formed by adding an –*ly* to a word, like this:

slow = slowly

rare = rarely

When a word ends with a –*y*, change the *y* to *i* and add –*ly*, like this:

happy = happily

noisy = noisily

Also, some adverbs cannot end with –*ly* such as:

again

never

sometimes

very

ever

now

already

quite

BUILDING SKILLS 8-3: Adding Adverbs

Add adverbs to the following sentences.

Example: The oldest neighbor on my street talks <u>quietly and shyly.</u>

1. The accused criminal spoke _____.

2. In the church, the chorus sang _____.

3. Marcus _____ answered the call.

4. Joe, the driver, drove _____.

5. The lone bird flew _____.

6. Write _____ and effectively.

7. Out of the hole, the snake slithered _____.

8. Minnie is leaving _____.

9. Paul _____ understood the complicated game.

10. At the ball, Robbie danced _____.

BUILDING SKILLS 8-4: Identifying Adverbs

Underline the adverbs in each sentence.

Example: She works <u>confidently</u> and meticulously on her science project.

1. Drew slowly and carefully turned his foot.

2. At the football game, the players played aggressively and defensively.

3. As everyone can see, Dave is extremely clumsy.

4. Jenny sleepily answered the phone.

5. Because he ran for two hours, the dog is very tired.

6. The room for the nursery is surprisingly sunny.

7. On Monday, the bad news came unexpectedly.

8. Jon was greatly concerned about the flood.

9. Maggie carefully unwrapped the mailed package.

10. The morning sunrise was startlingly bright.

BUILDING SKILLS 8-5: Writing Adjectives and Adverbs in Sentences

Add adjectives and adverbs to the following sentences.

Example: The minister addressed his congregation.

The wise, solemn minister eloquently addressed his loyal congregation.

1. A truck careened.

_____

2. Johnny, the singer, sang a song.

_____

3. A dog chased a cat.

_____

4. The child ran home.

_____

5. My boss gave me a raise.

_____

COMMON MISTAKES WITH ADJECTIVES AND ADVERBS

Some writers use adjectives when they need an adverb.

Answer me honest.

To be correct, the sentence should be:

Answer me honestly.

The word _honestly_ describes how the answer should be given; therefore, it is an adverb. The word _honest_ in the first sentence is really an adjective and if it must be used, then it should be placed so that it modifies the noun in the sentence:

Give me an honest answer.

Honest now comes before a noun—_answer_—and describes it.

BUILDING SKILLS 8-6: Changing Adjectives into Adverbs

In each sentence, change the bolded adjective in to an adverb.

Example: The **bright** light shines.

The light shines brightly.

1. The officer gave a **polite** reply.

   _____

2. The mechanic gave my car a **complete** check.

   _____

3. Mike has a **beautiful** voice when he sings.

   _____

4. The politician has an **aggressive** way of debating.

   _____

5. Anna wore a **simple** dress.

   _____

COMPARATIVE AND SUPERLATIVE FORMS

Adjectives and adverbs come in three different forms and are used to show degrees of comparison: **positive, comparative,** and **superlative.**

The **positive** form talks about one person or thing and maintains the initial form of the word.

> Brandon's puppy grew <u>fast</u>.
> Government spending is <u>wasteful</u>.

The **comparative** form presents two elements and makes a judgment between the two.

> Brandon's puppy grew <u>faster</u> than Jarod's puppy.
> Government spending is <u>more wasteful</u> this year than in previous years.

The **superlative** form presents or implies three or more elements, and makes a judgment that puts one on top.

> Of all the puppies we saw that day, Brandon's was <u>the fastest</u>.
> Government spending was <u>the least wasteful</u> in the area of highway safety and maintenance.

Showing degrees of comparison with adjectives and adverbs requires learning a few rules and concepts. You need to know that adjectives and adverbs can be either regular or irregular.

Regular Adjectives and Adverbs

When forming **regular modifiers,** follow these two rules:

- Use _–er_ or _more_ to form the comparative degree and _–est_ or _most_ to form the superlative degree of most one- and two-syllable modifiers.
- Use _more_ and _most_ to form the comparative and superlative degrees of all modifiers with three or more syllables.

Positive (1)	Comparative (2)	Superlative (3 or more)
tall	taller than	the tallest
thin	thinner than	the thinnest
fast	faster than	the fastest
dry	drier than	the driest
happy	happier than	the happiest
lovely	lovelier than	the loveliest
funny	funnier than	the funniest
beautiful	more beautiful than	the most beautiful
careful	more careful than	the most careful
intelligent	more intelligent than	the most intelligent
quickly	more quickly than	the most quickly
slender	more slender than	the most slender

Note: If a word ends with *–y*, you replace the *–y* with an *i* and you add an *–er* or an *–est* like:

pretty   →   prettier   →   prettiest

If an *–er* cannot be added to the comparative form, the word must take a *more,* and you cannot have both an *–er* ending a *more* added to the word. It is an "either/or" situation.

If the word takes an *–er* ending in comparative form, it will take an *–est* ending in superlative. On the other hand, if the word takes a *more* in comparative form then it would take a *most* in superlative form.

👆 MEMORY TIP

The **comparative form** of adjectives and adverbs requires adding either -er to the ending of the word OR *more* added to the positive form of the word.

> Elsa is <u>happier</u> than her sister Erin, but Erin is <u>more beautiful</u> than Elsa.

The **superlative form** requires adding either an -est to the ending of the word OR a *most* added to the positive form of the word. It also frequently takes "the" at the beginning.

> Among my ten cousins, Elsa is <u>the happiest</u>, but Erin is <u>the most beautiful</u>.

BUILDING SKILLS 8-7: Comparatives and Superlatives Forms

Write the comparative and superlative form of each adjective or adverb.

Example:	comparative	superlative
short	shorter	shortest

1. famous

2. lazy

3. decent

4. bright

5. wonderful

6. sad

7. ugly

8. fun

9. lonely

10. nice

11. terrible

12. skillful

13. rich

14. big

15. successful

Irregular Adjectives and Adverbs

Some adjectives are irregular in the way they change to show comparison. They are unique in that they form entirely new words in the comparative and superlative forms.

Positive	Comparative	Superlative
little*	less	least
many	more	most
far	farther/further	farthest/furthest

*Note: When *little* refers to quantity (a little hungry/less hungry/least hungry), it is irregular, but when *little* refers to physical size (a little puppy/a littler puppy/the littlest puppy), it is regular.

MEMORY TIP

Commonly confused words:

- Farther shows physical distance.

  My home is <u>farther</u> down the road.

- Further means "in addition" or "additional."

  I need <u>further</u> data for this survey.

BUILDING SKILLS 8-8: Choosing the Correct Comparative or Superlative Forms

Underline the appropriate comparative or superlative form of the adjective/adverb:

Example: Their mountain log cabin is (<u>older</u>, oldest) than ours.

1. That pine tree is the (tallest, taller) one in the grove.

2. His blonde curly hair is (longer, more long) than mine.

3. This is the (mildest, most mild) chili sauce I have found.

4. Everyone knows that Josh is (funner, more fun) than Matty.

5. That blue cashmere sweater is the (most beautiful, beautifullest) I have ever seen.

6. This small lamp is (brighter, more bright) than the other one.

7. Ron needs to obtain (further, farther) information from the agitated suspect.

8. The (less/least) coffee I consume, the (better, best) I feel.

9. Of all his five siblings, Jon is the (taller, tallest) one.

10. Bob is the (most daring, daringest) of the three boys.

FOUR MORE TRICKY ADJECTIVES AND ADVERBS

Perhaps the most irregular and often misused adjectives and adverbs are *good, bad, well,* and *badly.* They are among the most frequently confused adjectives and adverbs.

The words *good* and *bad* are always adjectives and often land before a noun. They answer the questions of *which one* and *what kind* of noun.

I am a good student.

The words *well* and *badly* are always adverbs and describe the verb or action in the sentence. They answer the question of *how* the verb is done.

> I study well.

Well describes the act of studying—how do I study? *Well* is often used with the verb *feel* when it means healthy as in *I feel well today*.

Wrong:	I did good on my test.
Right:	I did well on my test.
Wrong:	I am a well piano player.
Right:	I am a good piano player.
Wrong:	I feel good today after being sick with the flu.
Right:	I feel well today after being sick with the flu.

In comparative and superlative forms, these irregular words change drastically:

	Positive	Comparative	Superlative
Adjective	good	better	best
Adjective	bad	worse	worst
Adverb	well	better	best
Adverb	badly	worse	worst

BUILDING SKILLS 8-9: Using Good, Well, Bad, and Badly

Underline the appropriate word in the following sentences.

Example: The music teacher at our school, Mrs. Jensen, is a (<u>good</u>, well) pianist.

1. To avoid salmonella poisoning, I always cook eggs (well/good).

2. At the end of every Monday, I always seem to have a (bad/badly) headache.

3. Drew's mom said that he is behaving (well/good) in his English class.

4. The coach commented that since they have been practicing more frequently, the baseball team has performed (good/well).

5. Amazingly, Scott did (well/good) on his science test.

6. Even though the question was hard, you answered it (good/well).

7. The Angels have a (good/well) pitching staff this year.

8. You will do (well/good) on the exam if you do not stress out.

9. Barry, the kindergarten teacher, sings (good/well) songs for little kids.

10. My delicate stomach is upset today, so I do not feel (good/well).

BUILDING SKILLS 8-10: Comparative and Superlative Forms for Good, Bad, Well, Badly

Underline the correct comparative or superlative form for these irregular adjectives/adverbs.

Example: Over the weekend, Bessie's sickness got (<u>worse</u>, worst), and she needed to go the hospital.

1. This is the (worse, worst) concert I have ever been to.

2. Jane did (good/better, best) on this math test than on the last one.

3. Between the two of them, Mike is the (better, best) pitcher.

4. My headache is (bad, worse, worst) today than yesterday.

5. This is the (good, best, better) pie I have ever tasted.

6. Among all three contestants, she is the (worse, worst) speaker.

7. Of all my days, last Monday was the (worse, worst) day.

8. After drinking four beers, the man felt (worse, worst).

9. Of the thirteen dancers, Katie is the (better, best) one.

10. I feel (better, best) about my decision.

❗ BUILDING SKILLS TOGETHER 8-1: Correcting Adjective and Adverb Use in Writing

Work in small groups to cross out the mistake(s) in each sentence and write in the correction(s) above the text.

1. I remember the well experience of buying my dog at the pet store.

2. It left me feeling most grateful than I thought I could ever feel.

3. Of the three dogs I saw that day, the one I bought was the bestest.

4. This dog, whom I called Beny, was the big, the most happy and the energeticest dog I've ever seen.

5. As soon as Beny was brought out into the petting room, he excited ran up to me and gentle laid at my feet.

6. He looked up at me with warmly golden brown eyes and soft licked my hand.

7. As I scratched his longly ears, I felt his most rich and most soft texture of his coat.

8. But underneath all this softness, he had the most leaner and stronger muscles.

9. I quick fell in love with Beny and wanted to take him home with me.

10. As I petted him, the pet store owner told me that Beny was bad mistreated by his previous owner.

11. I wanted to hold him tight and chase away all his badly memories.

12. As I looked into his beautifullest eyes, I knew that Beny and I were going to get along good.

13. Since I wanted a fur friend so bad and since Beny and I hit it off good, I decided to adopt him.

14. Ever since, Beny and I have been inseparably, and I look forward to coming home to him every day.

15. I am gratefuller to know Beny's love for me.

✦ BUILDING SKILLS TOGETHER 8-2: Adjectives and Adverbs in Writing

Work in small groups on underlining the adjectives and circling the adverbs in this passage.

(1) The old lady settled herself comfortably, removing her white cotton gloves and putting them up with her purse on the shelf in front of the back window. (2) The children's mother still had on slacks and still had her head tied up in a green kerchief, but the grandmother had on a navy blue straw sailor hat with a bunch of white violets on the brim and a navy blue dress with a small white dot in the print. (3) Her collars and cuffs were white organdy trimmed with lace and at her neckline she had pinned a purple spray of cloth violets containing a sachet. (4) In case of an accident, anyone seeing her dead on the highway would know at once that she was a lady.

(5) She said she thought it was going to be a good day for driving, neither too hot nor too cold, and she cautioned Bailey that the speed limit was fifty-five miles an hour and that the patrolmen hid themselves behind billboards and small clumps of trees and sped out after you before you had a chance to slow down. (6) She pointed out interesting details of the scenery: Stone Mountain; the blue granite that in some places came up to both sides of the highway; the brilliant red clay banks slightly streaked with purple; and the various crops that made rows of green lace-work on the ground. (7) The trees were full of

silver-white sunlight and the meanest of them sparkled. (8) The children were reading comic magazines and their mother had gone back to sleep.

—From Flannery O'Connor, *"A Good Man is Hard to Find"*

CHAPTER EIGHT SKILLS REVIEW: Adjectives and Adverbs

A. Underline the adjectives and circle the adverbs in each sentence.

1. The old abandoned house stood proudly at the end of the long street.

2. That attractive, happy couple is obviously newly married.

3. The sleek cat perched gracefully onto the window seat.

B. Insert the appropriate adverb for each sentence.

4. The boisterous children played (loud) _____.

5. The charismatic politician was greeted (warm) _____.

6. The excited fans cheered (wild) _____.

C. Spot the adjective or adverb in the sentences below and write the form used: positive, comparative, or superlative.

7. That apartment building is the tallest in the area. _____

8. The lasagna is tasty. _____

9. Today's weather is warmer than yesterday. _____

10. My office is cleaner than yours. _____

11. The food is hot. _____

D. Write the comparative or superlative form of the adjective/adverb in each sentence.

12. Tim is reading the (thick) _____ book on the shelf.

13. This dress is (pretty) _____ than I expected.

14. Let us finish the job (quickly) _____ than Bill.

15. The new president gave a (short) _____ speech this time.

16. That movie is the (funny) _____ one of the season.

E. Underline the appropriate form of the adjective/adverb in the sentences.

17. Sonny skated (well, better, best) than Jenny.

18. This is the (worse, worst, bad) storm of the season.

19. This year's Christmas program is (good, better, best) than last year.
20. This test is (bad, worse, worst) than the one we had last week.
21. The dog's bark is (worse, worst) than his bite.
22. The fans behaved (bad, badly).
23. That (bad, badly) girl will not stop screaming!
24. He (bad, badly) wanted to go to the beach.
25. Jon had a (bad, badly) hiking experience.

CHAPTER NINE: The Ninth Building Block
Using Modifiers Correctly

You learned that adding descriptive details to your writing gives the reader a richer and more colorful idea of what you are discussing. The world of words would be a very boring place without adjectives and adverbs! However, a truth you may have discovered in other subjects, and in general life, is also true in grammar: The more ingredients or elements we add, the more opportunities we create for confusion and misunderstanding. Adjectives and adverbs—along with other modifiers like prepositional phrases—have such descriptive power that shifting where they are placed in a sentence can alter their meaning significantly.

The doctor <u>from Ohio</u> uploaded a video lecture on teenage criminals.

The doctor uploaded a video lecture on teenage criminals <u>from Ohio</u>.

The doctor uploaded a video lecture <u>from Ohio</u> on teenage criminals.

Notice how, as you read each sentence, your picture of the event changes. It is essential to understand how modifier placement—our ninth building block—affects the grammar of the sentence. Learning to control the effect of these powerful descriptors is a step forward for any writer. The first step is recognizing how the placement of a modifier creates confusion or wrong meaning. Modifiers are words, phrases, or clauses that provide description in sentences. **Misplaced** and **dangling modifiers** are the names grammar gives to modifier placement errors in sentences.

MISPLACED MODIFIERS

Adjectives and adverbs can never stand alone. *Pale blue. Hurriedly. Ever after. Large.* These modifiers require a subject and a verb if they are to become a grammatically functioning sentence. In addition, adjectives and adverbs must stay close to the noun or verb they are describing, or, like little children straying too far from their parents, these parts of speech will bring chaos and confusion.

John saw the Grand Canyon flying over Arizona.

What is happening in this sentence? At first glance, you might think the sentence is saying that the Grand Canyon was flying—but that cannot be right! Reading the sentence again, you might decide that John is in an airplane, flying over Arizona, looking down at the Grand Canyon. However, the sentence must be rewritten if you want to be completely certain. The modifier *flying over Arizona* is too far away from its subject; it is, therefore, a **misplaced modifier**. To fix this error, the modifier must be moved closer to the subject, *John*.

John, flying over Arizona, saw the Grand Canyon.

Another way to fix this is to add a conjunction and a pronoun, and change the sentence to one of the four correct kinds of sentences: simple, compound, complex, or compound-complex. There are several correct ways to add a conjunction and a pronoun to the original sentence. Notice that in each of the rewritten sentence, the modifier has been placed much closer to the subject.

<u>When</u> John was flying over Arizona, <u>he</u> saw the Grand Canyon.
John was flying over Arizona, <u>and</u> <u>he</u> saw the Grand Canyon.
John was flying over Arizona; therefore <u>he</u> saw the Grand Canyon.

✋ MEMORY TIP

To correct **misplaced modifiers**:

- Move the modifier closer to the subject it is modifying in the sentence.
  The waiter served a piece of bread to the woman that was well-buttered.

As it is written, this sentence implies that the woman is well-buttered when it should be the piece of bread.

- Add a conjunction and/or a pronoun to restructure the sentence as one of the four kinds of sentences: simple, compound, complex, or compound-complex.

Correct: **The waiter served the woman a piece of well-buttered bread.**

Correct: **When the piece of bread was well-buttered, the waiter served it to the woman.**

BUILDING SKILLS 9-1: Misplaced Modifiers

Determine if these sentences are correct or if they contain misplaced modifiers. Circle the appropriate answer.

1. I admired the sweater Samantha was wearing with happy flowers.
   a. Correct
   b. Misplaced Modifier

2. I like the sweater I bought at the store with puffed shoulders.
   a. Correct
   b. Misplaced Modifier

3. A swim in the pool feels good on a hot summer day.
   a. Correct
   b. Misplaced Modifier

4. Joanne gave all the books to her sister that she did not want anymore.
   a. Correct
   b. Misplaced Modifier

5. The colorful fish were appealing to the children in the twenty-gallon tank.
   a. Correct
   b. Misplaced Modifier

6. The fans clapping loudly cheered for their team.
   a. Correct
   b. Misplaced Modifier

7. I hope you realize that smoking causes cancer.
   a. Correct
   b. Misplaced Modifier

8. We stopped the truck hearing the police siren.
   a. Correct
   b. Misplaced Modifier

9. The jogger crossed the finish line wheezing to catch his breath.
   a. Correct
   b. Misplaced Modifier

10. My teacher failing the algebra test recommended a tutor to me.
    a. Correct
    b. Misplaced Modifier

BUILDING SKILLS 9-2: Misplaced Modifiers

Some of the following sentences contain misplaced modifiers. Identify the correct sentences by writing *S* and for the sentences with misplaced modifiers write *MM*. Rewrite the sentences that have misplaced modifiers.

Example: <u>MM</u> The dealer sold the new car to the buyer with leather seats.
   <u>The dealer sold the new car with leather seats to the buyer.</u>

_____ 1. We saw the plane had crashed on the living room television.

_____ 2. The truck was taken to the mechanic shop with a big flat tire.

_____ 3. Mrs. Smyth with a metal bottom sat in a chair.

_____ 4. The thief mugged the old lady with a masked and hooded face.

_____ 5. Jason changed his answers on the test.

_____ 6. I saw the keys walking down the alley.

_____ 7. The rider was thrown by the horse wearing red boots.

_____ 8. The man in the rocking chair sat by the big dog smoking his favorite pipe.

_____ 9. If you had listened to me, your term paper would be done by now.

_____ 10. The doctor asked me if I could move my legs falling from the tree.

DANGLING MODIFIERS

As writers seek to add interest and complexity to their writing, they need to make sure every action and descriptor they add is accurately tied to a logical subject. Without close attention, **misplaced modifiers** can crop up, along with another common error, the **dangling modifier**. Like a child who has let go of his parent's hand and is wandering around aimlessly, a dangling modifier occurs when a logical subject cannot be found to connect to a modifier in the sentence.

> Running to catch the bus, my wallet fell out of my coat.

Was the wallet running to catch the bus? Is that possible? We do not know who is running to catch the bus, and the nouns—*wallet* and *coat*—in the rest of the sentence cannot be the ones doing the running. To correct this dangling modifier:

1. Add a subject to the first part of the sentence, so the modifier words— *running to catch the bus*—belong to a specific and logical subject.
2. Sometimes you need to add more than a subject to the dangling modifier. You might need to add a verb and/or a conjunction, so the sentence is correctly structured.

   Clear: As I was running to catch the bus, my wallet fell out of my coat.

   Clear: I was running to catch the bus, but my wallet fell out of my coat.

   Clear: I ran to catch the bus; I felt my wallet fly out of my coat.

 MEMORY TIP

To correct dangling modifiers:

- Add a subject and, if necessary, a conjunction and a verb, to the sentence, making sure these additions are placed close to the problematic modifier.

Incorrect: When sixteen years old, Tom enrolled in medical school.

Correct: When Tom was sixteen years old, he enrolled in medical school.

BUILDING SKILLS 9-3: Dangling Modifiers

Determine if these sentences are correct or if they contain dangling modifiers. Circle the appropriate answer.

1. Peeking into the bag, the cookies were crushed.
   a. Correct
   b. Dangling Modifier

2. To obtain a loan from the bank, good credit is required.
   a. Correct
   b. Dangling Modifier

3. The driver turned the car on after the battery finished charging.
   a. Correct
   b. Dangling Modifier

4. While talking on the cell phone, the chef prepared my lunch.
   a. Correct
   b. Dangling Modifier

5. Stomping the ground, Timothy ran from the angry bull.
   a. Correct
   b. Dangling Modifier

6. We wished to purchase a travel package to Mexico.
   a. Correct
   b. Dangling Modifier

7. Barking loudly, the owner greeted the excited dog.
   a. Correct
   b. Dangling Modifier

8. Falling in love with Brad Pitt, Angelina Jolie was the envy of many people.
   a. Correct
   b. Dangling Modifier

9. Watching the show, the puppy sat on grandma's lap.
   a. Correct
   b. Dangling Modifier

10. While I waited for my date to show up, I talked to two of my friends.
    a. Correct
    b. Dangling Modifier

BUILDING SKILLS 9-4: Dangling Modifiers

Some of the following sentences contain dangling modifiers. For the correct sentences, write S and for the ones with dangling modifiers write DM. Rewrite the sentences that have dangling modifiers.

Example: <u>DM</u> Having been fixed the night before, Pam could use her bicycle.
<u>After her bicycle was fixed, Pam used it to go to school.</u>

➡

_____ 1. To earn an *A*, many hours of study are needed.

_____ 2. At the age of four, my sister Marie was born.

_____ 3. Being a good parent, endless patience is needed.

_____ 4. You must complete all the requirements if you want to graduate by June.

_____ 5. Waiting for the bus, the snow started falling.

_____ 6. Baked in butter, Len served the lobster.

_____ 7. To run in the marathon, many hours of practice are needed.

_____ 8. Sailing in stormy waters, seasickness took over the passengers.

_____ 9. Falling off the table, Tom reached for the jar of pickles.

_____ 10. Driving a small car, parking spaces can be a problem.

Misplaced and dangling modifiers often make very funny word pictures:

Incorrect: I glimpsed a rat sorting the recyclable materials.
Correct: I glimpsed a rat <u>as I was</u> sorting the recyclable materials.

Incorrect: We saw a great blue heron on vacation in Canada.
Correct: <u>While we were</u> on vacation in Canada, we saw a great blue heron.

As you complete the exercises, enjoy the humor, and use it to help you recognize placement errors.

🕯 BUILDING SKILLS TOGETHER 9-1: Modifiers in Writing

Working with a partner, read the following paragraph and identify the modifier problems. Correct the errors by rewriting the sentences.

(1) I worry about my 8-year-old sister Lori because she only talks to one person, her imaginary friend, Mary. (2) At age four, their friendship developed. (3) Talking to Mary constantly, Lori darts around everyone full of energy. (4) Lori can't seem to get close besides Mary to anyone. (5) Shutting Mom, Dad, and me out, Lori has no other friends. (6) Lori needs to establish some connection with real people around her. (7) While learning to trust others, more normalcy and security can be found for Lori. (8) I am committed to helping my sister with real people have healthy relationships.

🕯 BUILDING SKILLS TOGETHER 9-2: Modifiers in Writing

Working with a small group, read the following essay and identify the modifier problems. Identify each sentence as *MM*, *DM*, or *Correct* and then rewrite the incorrect sentences.

A Day in the Life of a Casino Manager

(1) Being a casino manager, none of my days are average. (2) Every day is different. (3) One day, for example, I am handling for Rod Stewart dinner reservations. (4) The next day, explaining to a member of a Hollywood entourage, the water fountain is not for swimming. (5) The next day, I am paying a life-changing jackpot to a customer over $1 million. (6) And on Friday, explaining to one of my best VIP customers, his dogs cannot stay in the hotel rooms even if they are considered to be like children. (7) Thinking I've seen it all, something always happens to remind me that anything is possible. (8) I learned early on never to say "Now I've seen it all."

(9) Working the day shift, I show up forty-five minutes before my shift begins to get debriefed on what occurred during the night shift. (10) I'm told the poker tournament had been an enormous success sponsored by a local radio

show. (11) Security out of the 600 tournament guests had only dealt with a couple of intoxicated guests. (12) I'm also told about the two players who had tried to cheat the casino by switching cards in table games. (13) Completing the paperwork to exclude these players, I work with the compliance manager.

(14) Just starting to check my e-mail, a large jackpot hit on the main casino floor. (15) The winners were a local poor couple. (16) I spend a few minutes celebrating with the fortunate customers.

(17) Two hours into it, catching up with employees on the floor, I head to a meeting with the marketing team. (18) The meeting from across the property involved managers focusing on promotions and events that will drive increased customers. (19) Later, having lunch with VIP customers, they are unhappy about being bumped out of a suite. (20) I knew the reality of the best suites gotten by the biggest players. (21) Taking care of lunch for my VIPs, I wished them good luck and left.

(22) By late afternoon early evening, I've signed paperwork for a large funds transfer and checked in on the table games to see how business was going.

(23) Complimenting the pit boss on managing the table limits, play was strong to match our business levels. (24) Security called with our nightclub on a domestic dispute. (25) Having arrived on the scene, our officers had everything under control. (26) It seemed a husband's choice of dancing partners was unhappy with his wife. (27) Not escalating into a physical confrontation, I let the security officers finish defusing the situation.

(28) I spend the last half hour of my shift debriefing the events of the day to my night shift counterpart. (29) I left for home knowing my leadership, management, and customer skills will challenge tomorrow's set of surprises.

—From Chon/Maier, *Welcome to Hospitality: An Introduction*

CHAPTER NINE SKILLS REVIEW: Dangling or Misplaced Modifiers

Identify the error and write *MM*, *DM*, or *Sentence* on the line next to each sentence. Then, rewrite the modified sentences.

_____ 1. Walking through the farm, the dog was excited.

_____ 2. I saw a scary monster watching a television show.

_____ 3. To avoid the traffic jam, a detour was encouraged.

_____ 4. I carefully unwrapped from my sister the colorful package.

_____ 5. The contestants kissed their loved ones covered with sweat.

_____ 6. Wearing a pink skirt, Ali was entertained by his date.

_____ 7. The pet owner went to the veterinarian with a sick hamster.

_____ 8. To be avoided at all cost, walking in the muddy water of the river.

_____ 9. When we left the campsite, we looked scruffy and sweaty.

_____ 10. Just returned from fabulous travel destinations, I felt like a famous explorer.

_____ 11. Scrambling through the front door, Bert reaches his car before his dad honks the horn.

_____ 12. The first rays of sun penetrate through the clouds and onto our front porch.

_____ 13. Reaching the point of no return, the soldiers aggressively fought the enemy.

_____ 14. The class worked hard to finish the group project on time.

_____ 15. Soaked to the bone, the men's boots came off at the door.

CHAPTER TEN: The Tenth Building Block
Parallelism

You read in a menu at a local restaurant, "In his cooking, our famous chef uses fresh ingredients, is preparing Italian dishes, and created culinary masterpieces" and think that it just does not sound quite right. You may be wondering why? There is a reason it sounds a bit off, and that is the writer has broken the parallelism rule. The correct way to write the above sentence is: "In his cooking, our famous chef uses the freshest ingredients, prepares Italian dishes, and creates culinary masterpieces." Chapter Ten introduces this important grammar rule: Whenever you repeatedly use a part of speech in a sentence, each use must consistently present the part of speech in the same form. This consistency is called **parallel construction,** or **parallelism**. Parallelism is all about equality and creating a nice rhythm in your sentences. It is the tenth building block in our study of grammar.

PARALLELISM

Parallelism in writing means that similar elements or ideas in a sentence are repeated or presented in the same form grammatically, so the reader can quickly and smoothly grasp the comparison or connection being made between them. Knowing the parts of speech is important for learning parallelism; you may wish to review Appendix A in conjunction with this chapter.

Incorrect: In my spare time, I like to read books, to watch documentaries, and attending seminars.

This sentence is not parallel because the items in the list are not all grammatically similar. Although infinitive verbs are listed, they are not all treated the same way.

Correct: In my spare time, I like to read books, to watch documentaries, and to attend seminars.

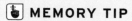

MEMORY TIP

The need for parallel construction arises when your sentence contains any of the following conditions:

- Pairs (two items)
- Lists (three or more items)
- Comparisons using *than* or *as*
- Paired expressions

Parallelism with Pairs

Pairs and lists require the use of parallel structure. You can spot pairs (two items) in sentences by looking for the following words: *and, or.*

I bought coffee <u>and</u> tea.
I bought coffee <u>or</u> tea.

When you use these two words, everything that comes before the and / or must present the same grammatical form as everything that comes after the and / or.

Incorrect: We can <u>go</u> to the beach <u>or</u> we <u>are going</u> to the park.

In this sentence, you can see that the verbs on either side of *or* are not the same grammatically. You need to change one of the sides to make the sentence parallel.

Correct: We <u>can go</u> to the beach <u>or</u> we <u>can go</u> to the park.
Correct: We <u>are going</u> to the beach <u>or</u> we <u>are going</u> to the park.
Correct: We can go <u>to the beach</u> <u>or</u> <u>to the park</u>.

As you can see, multiple options exist for creating parallelism in any sentence.

Incorrect: He dances <u>skillfully</u> <u>and</u> <u>with gracefulness</u>.

Here, the adverb *skillfully* comes before the *and* while the noun *gracefulness* comes after the *and*. The sentence will not achieve parallelism until one of these modifiers is changed.

Correct: He dances <u>skillfully</u> <u>and</u> <u>gracefully</u>. [adverb / adverb]
Correct: He dances <u>with skill</u> <u>and</u> <u>grace</u>. [noun / noun]

Parallelism with Lists

Parallelism must be achieved whenever lists occur in a sentence, no matter what parts of speech are involved. A list includes more than three items. All items in a list must be constructed in the same grammatical manner.

Put commas between items in a list. When giving a short and simple list of things in a sentence, the last comma (right before *and* or *or*) is optional, but it is never wrong. If the items in the list are longer and more complicated, you should always place a final comma before *and/or*.

A good student listens attentively to his teachers, reads frequently, and writes properly.

Here are some rules to keep in mind for keeping lists parallel.

1. **Pairs and lists of <u>verbs</u> must be parallel in tense.**

   On my birthday, we sang, danced, and were eating.

   The list in this example starts with a past tense of the verb *sang;* all the verbs listed after *sang,* therefore, should also be in the past tense. *Were eating* is in the progressive past; hence, this sentence is not parallel. To correct the sentence, either change *were eating* to *ate* or change all the other verbs to past progressive:

   Correct: **On my birthday, we sang, danced, and ate.**
   Correct: **On my birthday, we were singing, dancing, and eating.**

   Note: In any list of items, be sure to use commas between each item.

2. **Pairs and lists of <u>nouns</u> must be parallel in number, person, and kind.**

   I bought coffee, some tea, and two pounds of sugar.

   The list in this example starts with a noun that has no designated measurement while the last two nouns have designated measurements. Hence, this list is not parallel. To correct the sentence, either add measurements to all the nouns or remove the measurements from all the nouns.

   Correct: **I bought coffee, tea, and sugar.**
   Correct: **I bought one pound of coffee, two pounds of tea, and two pounds of sugar.**

3. **Pairs and lists of <u>adjectives</u> must be parallel in form.**

   The race was dangerous, creative, and had much excitement.

   The list in this example has an inappropriate adjective *(had much excitement)* which does not parallel the treatment of the other two adjectives in the sentence. Hence, this list is not parallel. To correct this sentence, reduce the last adjective to one word.

   Correct: **The race was a dangerous, creative, and exciting.**

BUILDING SKILLS 10-1: Parallelism with Pairs and Lists

Determine if the following sentences are parallel. Next to each sentence, write *P* for parallel or *NP* for nonparallel.

Example: <u>NP</u> The secretary was asked to write his report quickly, accurately, and in a thorough manner.

_____ 1. My brother likes building tree houses and to collect unique rocks.

_____ 2. I spend my weekends cleaning my apartment or to do laundry.

_____ 3. Our dog likes to swim, fetching, and to walk.

_____ 4. Baseball and playing tennis are good ways to have fun.

_____ 5. I ran errands, cleaned, and had to cook today.

_____ 6. I know someone who does not eat meat and avoids wheat.

_____ 7. The perfect cake is moist and tastes good.

_____ 8. She has a pretty face and is very charming.

_____ 9. A headache can be an inconvenience or a serious problem.

_____ 10. I had fun dancing, singing, and games.

_____ 11. I like to listen to my iPod, watching old movies, and run in the park.

_____ 12. Bonnie spent two hours planning the picnic and bought groceries.

_____ 13. The college catalog showed a different room, time, and teacher for my course.

_____ 14. He needs to choose to go to California or staying at home.

_____ 15. The cat was playing with the string and ran around the bedroom.

BUILDING SKILLS 10-2: Parallelism and Lists

Rewrite the following nonparallel sentences.

Example: On the weekends, Mona likes hiking, to swim, and riding a bicycle.

<u>On the weekends, Mona likes hiking, swimming, and bike riding.</u>

1. My mother did the cleaning, ironing, and cooked when I was a child.

_____

_____

2. I am thankful for my health, my family, and for having a job.

_____

_____

3. Many think that running is boring and that it is tiring.

_____

_____

4. Rachel is sweet, smart, and she has good manners.

_____

_____

5. Hiking, fishing, and to camp require a love of the outdoors.

_____

_____

Parallelism in Comparisons (*Than* or *As*)

To make comparisons, you must use the words *than* or *as*. When you edit for parallelism, make sure that the items being compared on either side of those words are parallel.

<u>Driving</u> to school is better than <u>to take</u> the bus.

The verbs on either side of *than* are not presented in the same tense. You must change one or the other to make the sentence parallel.

Correct: Driving to school is better <u>than</u> taking the bus.
Correct: To drive to school is better <u>than</u> to take the bus.

BUILDING SKILLS 10-3: Parallelism and Comparison

Determine if the following sentences are parallel. Next to each sentence, write *P* for parallel or *NP* for nonparallel.

Example: <u>NP</u> My father always cautioned that it is better to admit a mistake than denying it.

_____ 1. They would rather go to the beach than to go to school.

_____ 2. The earth revolves around the sun as well as it is spinning on its axis.

_____ 3. Gerri enjoys dancing at clubs more than to attend the opera.

_____ 4. Studying chemistry is as frustrating as to study algebra.

_____ 5. Ed is known more for his persistence in studying than his attention in class.

_____ 6. She likes reading stories as much as to watch television.

_____ 7. To love someone is better than to have never loved anyone.

_____ 8. Cooking is as much fun as to clean the house.

_____ 9. Admitting to a mistake is better than to deny it.

_____ 10. The engaged couple prefer going to the movie theaters than to watch television.

BUILDING SKILLS 10-4: Parallelism and Comparisons

Rewrite the following nonparallel sentences so that they are parallel.

Example: It will be slower to go this way than going that way.

> It will be slower to go this way than to go that way.

1. Listening to the morning lecture on plants was more interesting than to listen to the boring afternoon lecture.

   _____

   _____

2. Running for thirty minutes every day is as good an exercise as to bicycle.

   _____

   _____

3. The farmers planted more trees this year than they were planting last year.

   _____

   _____

4. Living on your own is harder than to live with family.

   _____

   _____

5. The invention of the computer is as important as inventing the telephone.

   _____

   _____

Parallelism with Paired Expressions

Paired expressions—also called correlative conjunctions—require parallel structure. These five sets of conjunctions are always paired:

> Both. . . and
>
> Either. . . or
>
> Neither . . .nor
>
> Not only. . . but also or but too
>
> Rather. . . than

🖐 MEMORY TIP

When using parallelism with paired expressions, the words after the first word are treated the same as the words after the second word.

       ↓   ↓

both _____ and _____

either _____ or _____

not only _____ but also _____

rather _____ than _____

Achieve parallel construction when using paired expressions by presenting the words that follow the first conjunction in the same format as the words that follow the second conjunction.

Example: I want <u>both to be wealthy and</u> health.
Correct: I want both to be wealthy and to be healthy.
Correct: I want both wealth and health.

Example: <u>Either we go</u> to the park <u>or we are going</u> to the mountains.
Correct: Either we go to the park or we go to the mountains.
Correct: Either we are going to the park or we are going to the mountains.

Example: He can <u>neither tell his</u> boss the truth <u>nor to quit his</u> job is possible.
Correct: He can neither tell his boss the truth nor quit his job.

Example: Sugar is used <u>not only in cakes but</u> to make <u>paste</u>.
Correct: Sugar is used not only in cakes but also in paste.
Correct: Sugar is used not only to make cakes but to make paste too.

Example: They would <u>rather eat out than to be eating their father's</u> cooking.
Correct: They would rather eat out than eat their father's cooking.

BUILDING SKILLS 10-5: Parallelism and Paired Expressions

Determine if the following sentences are parallel, and next to each sentence, write *P* for parallel or *NP* for nonparallel.

Example: <u>NP</u> At the party, not only was he rude, but also ate all the meatballs.

_____ 1. Not only does Thomas ask many questions, but he is always repeating what everyone says.

_____ 2. Regis will either have to study agriculture or he will be studying accounting.

_____ 3. Alex will succeed at his goal because of both his commitment and he has persistence.

_____ 4. Denis knew neither what to put on his application nor what to say in his resume.

_____ 5. We not only went camping, but we were wanting to raft down the raging river.

_____ 6. The mechanic changed both the broken gearbox and the oil needed changing.

_____ 7. Aunt Sammy was both surprised by and angered by my request for money.

_____ 8. Either order the computer parts on the Internet or by calling the toll-free number.

_____ 9. Tess would rather travel to Florida than to stay with her family.

_____ 10. James not only entertained the guest with jokes, but he also sang songs.

BUILDING SKILLS 10-6: Parallelism and Paired Expressions

Rewrite the following nonparallel sentences to correct them.

Example: I neither have finished the book nor wrote the report.

<u>I have neither finished the book nor written the report.</u>

1. I want both freedom and to be rich.

_____

_____

2. My fiancé is not only ambitious, but also looks good.

   _____

   _____

3. Tim would rather do the gardening than cleaning the house.

   _____

   _____

4. Either we buy the pecan pie or we are buying the pumpkin pie.

   _____

   _____

5. This movie is neither educational nor was I entertained by it.

   _____

   _____

BUILDING SKILLS 10-7: Writing Parallel Sentences

Complete the following sentences with parallel words, phrases, or clauses.

1. At the bowling alley, we can _____, _____, and _____.

2. I use my laptop for both _____ and _____.

3. A student needs four qualities to succeed in college: _____, _____, _____, and _____.

4. They would rather _____ than _____.

5. I am not only good at _____ but also at _____.

6. He will either _____ or _____.

7. They not only _____ but _____ too.

8. When I lay down for an afternoon nap, I am _____, _____, and _____.

9. My dream vacation would be to go to _____ or _____.

10. Her prom dress was _____, _____ and _____.

BUILDING SKILLS TOGETHER 10-1: Parallelism and Writing

Work with a partner or a small group and review these passages for parallel structures. Next to each number, write *P* for parallel or *NP* for nonparallel and then revise the *NP* sentences.

A Bravery Gene?

(1) Anxiety and being fearful have been felt by every human being. (2) However, some individuals are so filled with anxiety or fearful they are not able to function within society. (3) For example, individuals with agoraphobia have an abnormal fear of being helpless in a situation from which they cannot escape, so they are staying in an environment in which they feel secure. (4) Many agoraphobic people never leave their homes and are avoiding all public or open places.

(5) Recently, scientists working with mice found that by removing a single gene, they could turn normally cautious animals into brave animals that are more willing to explore an unknown territory or not being intimidated by dangers. (6) By analyzing brain tissue, scientists located a gene in a tiny prune-shaped region of the brain called amygdala, an area of the brain that is extremely active when animals or humans are being afraid or anxiety. (7) This gene produces a protein called stathmin. (8) Tests in the breed of mice that had that gene removed was twice as willing to explore unknown territories as the mice with the gene still in them. (9) In addition, when the mice were trained to expect a small electrical shock after being presented with a stimulus such as a sound or sight, this group of mice did not seem as being afraid when the sight or sound was given.

(10) Researchers are theorizing that stathmin helps form fearful memories in the amygdala of the brain, the area where fears seem to be stored. (11) If the production of stathmin can be halted or inhibiting it by medication, it is possible that fears would not be stored as unconscious memories. (12) This would greatly decrease an individual's anxieties. (13) Think of all the people whose lives are affected by anxiety and fearfulness.

(14) With this medication, not only will these anxieties and fears be decreased or eliminated, but these people are leading normal healthy lives.

—From Louise Simmers, *Introduction to Health Science Technology*

1. _____   8. _____

2. _____   9. _____

3. _____   10. _____

4. _____   11. _____

5. _____   12. _____

6. _____   13. _____

7. _____   14. _____

CHAPTER TEN SKILLS REVIEW: Parallelism

For each sentence, circle the sentence that is parallel.

1. a) Good students need to attend class, be taking notes, and study hard.
   b) Good students need to attend class, to take notes, and to study hard.

2. a) My chores include picking up the laundry and to wash the dishes after dinner.
   b) My chores include picking up the laundry and washing the dishes after dinner.

3. a) I prefer cooking vegetarian dishes than cooking meat dishes.
   b) I prefer cooking vegetarian dishes than to cook meat dishes.

4. a) Our new car has both comfortable seats and a spacious interior.
   b) Our new car has both comfortable seats and it has lots of inside space.

5. a) Advertisers use either scary commercials to sell products or are using humor to sell products.
   b) Advertisers either use scary tactics or humor in commercials.

6. a) Not only did Farmer Bob feed the pigs but he was milking the cows.
   b) Not only did Farmer Bob feed the pigs, but he also milked the cows.

7. a) At summer camp, we spend our time hiking, swimming, and bowling.

    b) At summer camp, we spend our times hiking, to swim, and we go bowling.

8. a) The party begins at seven and eleven is when it is ending.

    b) The party begins at seven and ends at eleven.

9. a) Women are judged by their beauty or intelligence.

    b) Women are judged by their beauty or being intelligent is also good.

10. a) I realized that the story is both educational and it had humor in it.

    b) I realized that the story is both educational and humorous.

11. a) An effective teacher must be demanding, understanding, and encouraging.

    b) An effective teacher must be demanding, understand the students, and give encouragement.

12. a) Many dieters use either the low-carbohydrate diet or they use the one with low protein intake.

    b) Many dieters use either the low-carbohydrate diet or the low protein diet.

13. a) At the gym, we take aerobic classes, we lift weights, and we do pilates.

    b) At the gym, we take aerobic classes, we're lifting weights, and we did pilates.

14. a) Either Manny prepares the meal himself or he sends out for take-out.

    b) Either Manny prepares the meal himself or he has to send for take-out.

15. a) I can neither condone nor will I accept the unfair proposal.

    b) I can neither condone nor accept the unfair proposal.

UNIT FIVE: Punctuation

CHAPTER ELEVEN: The Eleventh Building Block
Comma Use

In Chapters One through Ten, you learned grammar's rules for how eight parts of speech can be combined in an endless number of creative yet orderly arrangements called sentences. The tiny curved mark called a **comma** plays an important role in helping the reader clearly follow the meaning in a sentence. Chapter Eleven shows you how to use commas to present strong sentences.

Commas are punctuation marks that signal readers to pause briefly when reading sentences. That pause helps readers understand the flow of thought or action. Beginning writers may use either too few or too many commas, so their sentences are unclear or difficult to read.

Six specific conditions require the use of commas. These conditions are divided into two categories: commas used to separate and commas used to enclose. Each category has three rules.

COMMAS USED TO SEPARATE

Commas create a necessary pause between two independent clauses, allowing readers time to separate and compare them in their minds. They are also used to create a small but necessary amount of separation between items in a list and phrases that introduce or lead up to an independent clause. There are three rules for commas that separate:

Rule # 1—Commas and Conjunctions

There are three types of conjunctions, and with each type, you must use commas in different locations to separate the clauses. (Refer to Memory Tip on conjunction use in Chapter Six on page 141.)

- Coordinating conjunctions (or FANBOYS) join two independent clauses and require a comma before the conjunction.

    John finished his essay, <u>but</u> Brian is still working on his.

- Adverbial conjunctions (or HOT SHOT MAMA CAT), join two or more independent clauses and require a semicolon before the conjunction and a comma after the conjunction.

    Kim went to the party; <u>however</u>, she did not stay long.

- Subordinating conjunctions (or WASBIT) join an independent clause with a dependent clause and require a comma only if the subordinating conjunction is at the beginning of the sentence.

    <u>When</u> I got home, I saw the mess the robbers had left behind.
    [Comma needed]

    I saw the mess the robbers had left behind <u>when</u> I got home.
    [Comma not needed]

 MEMORY TIP

Remember the acronyms for the types of conjunctions and how commas work with them:

Coordinating conjunctions	, FANBOYS
Adverbial conjunctions	; HOT SHOT MAMA CAT,
Subordinating conjunctions	WASBIT +DC, IC

BUILDING SKILLS 11-1: Commas and Conjunctions

Read each sentence carefully and insert commas where needed after you identify the type of conjunction in each sentence using the following:
- Coordinating Conjunction (or FANBOYS)
- Adverbial Conjunction (or HOT SHOT MAMA CAT)
- Subordinating Conjunction (or WASBIT)

Example: We knew the tornado had passed for the house stopped trembling.
*for*____Coordinating Conjunction_____

1. I like roast beef but I have grown tired of it.

_____

2. Sean joined the basketball team; however he often missed practice.

_____

3. Trey and Luis sang in the choir while Sam played in the band.

_____

4. When the storm hit, we hid in the basement.

_____

5. We had not finished our group project; nevertheless, we went to the movie theater.

_____

6. Would you rather fail the class, or would you rather drop it altogether?

_____

7. That car is quite handsome; nonetheless, it is too expensive.

_____

8. My favorite season is fall, but my kids like summer best of all.

_____

9. The lawn needs mowing; on the other hand, the weeds need pulling.

_____

10. Although some people become famous, they often have humble beginnings.

_____

- -

◆ BUILDING SKILLS TOGETHER 11-1: Conjunctions and Commas

With a partner, read each sentence carefully and insert commas where needed after you identify the type of conjunction in each sentence using the following:

- Coordinating Conjunction (or FANBOYS)
- Adverbial Conjunction (or HOT SHOT MAMA CAT)
- Subordinating Conjunction (or WASBIT)

1. Commas are punctuation marks and they signal the reader to pause when reading sentences.

_____

2. The pause created by the comma permits the reader to take a deep breath so that it allows oxygen to the brain and helps with comprehension.

_____

3. Writers either avoid using commas or overuse commas so their sentences are unclear or difficult to read.

_____

4. Since there are specific rules for comma use the writer must adhere to them in order to communicate effectively.

_____

5. Commas could be used to separate words or clauses on the other hand they could be used to enclose words or phrases.

_____

6. The meaning of a sentence is often clarified by a comma in the right place.

_____

7. A comma joins independent clauses however it comes before a coordinating conjunction in the middle of the sentence.

_____

8. If an adverbial conjunction is used to bring clauses together the comma goes after the conjunction before the second clause.

_____

9. If a subordinating conjunction is used at the beginning of the sentence a comma must be used at the end of the dependent clause.

_____

10. A comma is not needed if the subordinating conjunction is between the two clauses.

_____

Rule # 2–Commas and Items in a List

Use commas to separate items in a list (three or more items). This includes the last item in the series which usually has either the word _and_ or the word _or_ before it.

Series of nouns: I bought coffee, tea, flour, and sugar.
Series of verbs: At the meeting, I ate, drank, and mingled with my supervisors.

 MEMORY TIP
Here is how commas look in a list:

Item, item, item, and item.

BUILDING SKILLS 11-2: Commas and Items in a List

Add commas where needed.

Example: My camping experience was exciting, challenging, and adventurous.

1. We have many storms in November December and January.

2. Sammy, Joanne, and Matilda fight all the time.

3. I have to take chemistry physics and geometry to graduate next year.

4. I stopped at the cleaners went to the grocery store and picked up the kids from school.

5. They packed their bags loaded the van and set out for the campsite.

6. The weather was awful; I did not know whether to take a windbreaker a sweater or a heavy coat.

7. In my bedroom, there is a television a computer and an iPod stereo.

8. The students from fourth sixth and seventh grade participated in the science fair.

9. I bought pants and a jacket the other day.

10. The teacher searched in his briefcase through the desk and around his office for his missing book.

Rule # 3—Commas and Introductory Expressions

An introductory expression is a phrase composed of one word (*finally, oh, however*) or a group of words (*by the end of the day* or *as we all know*). It comes at the beginning of a sentence, and it never contains the subject and verb that create the basic meaning of the sentence. In other words, if you were to take the introductory expression out of the sentence, the remaining part of the sentence would make sense on its own. Use a comma after an introductory expression to let your readers know which part of the sentence is the main one or the one that makes sense on its own.

> Nonetheless, I must take this in to the inspector.
>
> By the way, I spoke to Tim today.
>
> According to Mr. Smith, the case is about to be closed.

 MEMORY TIP

Here is what commas look like with introductory expressions:

Introductory expression,   main sentence or clause.

BUILDING SKILLS 11-3: Commas with Introductory Expressions

Add commas where needed.

Example: Undoubtedly◎ interviewing for a new job is a stressful experience.

1. First find the magnifying glass.

2. Suddenly the thunder clapped and the lightning struck.

3. Because of the pain he wanted to go to the emergency room.

4. After two hours of waiting the mayor finally gave his speech.

5. Before leaving class the student checked his bag for his books.

6. In total darkness the thief went through the safe and stole the jewelry.

7. Finally you have arrived just when we needed you.

8. By the way I did not know your connection to the police.

9. As a matter of fact he was put in jail for 40 years.

10. Before a job interview you should practice with someone.

 MEMORY TIP

There are three rules for commas that separate:

1. with conjunctions
2. with lists
3. with introductory expressions

COMMAS TO ENCLOSE

Words or phrases that are not essential to the basic understanding of a sentence must be enclosed, or surrounded, by commas.

Rule # 4–Commas and Interrupters

An **interrupter** is a word or a group of words that appears in the middle of the sentence but which, like an introductory expression, does not contain the subject or verb necessary to the basic meaning of the sentence. Interrupters may separate the subject and the verb and may break the sentence's flow sometimes for dramatic effect, but they can be removed or "scooped out," and the sentence would retain its meaning. In short, interrupters do not add to or subtract from the basic grammatical meaning of a sentence.

Beth, a senior in high school, will finish her project on time.

If you strike out the interrupter that separates the subject from the verb, the sentence still makes sense.

Beth, ~~a senior in high school,~~ will finish her project on time.

The basic meaning of the sentence is *Beth will finish her project on time.*

 MEMORY TIP

Remember that interrupters are nonessential words to grasping the main information of the sentence. They can be removed or scooped out, and if they are, the sentence retains its complete meaning. Since they can be removed or "scooped out," it may be easier to think of them as "scoopables." Here is what scoopables look like with commas:

Subject, Scoopable, Verb

Use commas before and after an interrupter or "scoopable" to enclose or set off from the "unscoopable" subject and verb of the sentence.

I must take this, <u>nonetheless</u>, and show it to the inspector.
I spoke to Tim, <u>by the way</u>, and he agreed to come.
The criminal case, <u>according to Mr. Smith</u>, is about to be closed.

BUILDING SKILLS 11-4: Commas and Interrupters

Add commas where needed.
Example: My boss⊙ for example⊙ has never taken a day of vacation.

1. The guests it seems are enjoying the food.

2. Dr. Westermore however came to California from Idaho.

3. You I believe are a menace to society!

4. Your proposal by the way was rejected.

5. My sister-in-law Tammy moved into our house last week.

6. Maria an English teacher works at a community college.

7. The lawyer Garth Benedict won the controversial murder case.

8. The concert I attended unfortunately was a huge disappointment.

9. The hurricane sadly caused two hundred deaths.

10. The president a young female gave a moving speech.

Rule # 5—Commas and Direct Address

When the speaker in a sentence talks to another person and names that person, the process is called direct address because the speaker is directly addressing his or her audience. Put commas around the name or title that appears in the sentence.

<u>John</u>, may I stop by your office today?

I think, <u>Sir</u>, you are mistaken about the situation.

Your grades are excellent, <u>Manny</u>!

 MEMORY TIP

If the name is the subject in the sentence, do not separate the subject from the verb with a comma unless there is an interrupter.

Incorrect: John, is my friend.

Correct: John is my friend.

Here, the sentence is talking *about* John, not to John, so the name is the subject in the sentence, and the subject cannot be separated from the verb with a comma.

BUILDING SKILLS 11-5: Commas with Direct Address

Add commas where needed.

Example: Mom⊙ is the cake ready for me to decorate?

1. Scott do you have time for a chat?

2. I cannot believe Yvonne that you failed that class.

3. It is a pleasure to give you this promotion Ella.

4. Allen your travel request has been denied.

5. Thank you dear for the wonderful coffee.

6. How often should my child take this medicine Doctor?

7. Do you think Iris that the Yankees will win this year?

8. I called you Mr. Ronson to tell you about the dire situation at the company.

9. Paul will you please stop that noise.

10. I must say Rebecca this case is puzzling.

Rule # 6—Commas with Dates and Addresses

Use a comma to separate the month and day from the year.

I was born on November 15, 2001.

November 15 is one day out of 365 days of the calendar year 2001. That is, it is one day inside of that year, so a comma is needed to separate the day from the year and to indicate that the specific day falls inside that specific year.

Also, if you include the name of a day in your date, separate it from the other elements with a comma.

I was elected on Tuesday, November 4, 2008.

If you write a sentence that includes the month, day, and year at the beginning, you must include a comma after the year:

On May 12, 2001, I found out about my father's cancer.

👆 MEMORY TIP

Do not use a comma if:

1. Just the month and year are given.

   I was elected in November 2008.

2. The date precedes the month

   I was born on 10 January 1996.

Here the month keeps the numbers separated, so no comma is needed.

Use a comma to separate the city from the state for an address in a sentence.

I lived in Dallas, Texas.

If the sentence continues after the state name, place a comma after the state.

I lived in Dallas, Texas, but I moved two years ago.

If the sentence includes the street address, city, and state as part of the sentence, each item of the address must be separated with commas.

He lives at 100 W. Pine Street, Covina, California 10012.

Notice the house number and street are not separated by a comma, nor are the state and zip code. If the sentence continues, you must separate the last item in the address from the rest of the sentence with another comma:

He lives at 100 W. Pine Street, Covina, California 10012, but he is thinking of moving soon.

Commas also separate countries from the city/state/province:

I have visited Edinburgh, Scotland, and Paris, France.

BUILDING SKILLS 11-6: Commas and Dates

Add commas where needed.

Example: On May 10ⓒ 2000ⓒ she quit her job.

1. Claudia was born on June 3 1983.

2. On September 15 2003 the destructive hurricane struck.

3. I last visited my grandmother on September 13 1988.

4. James and Betty were married on October 23 1975.

5. I bought this house in May 2000.

6. During July 1999 I was working at The Home Depot as a cashier.

7. Connor won the Madden championship on August 2 2002.

8. I still remember the day I met the love of my life; it was on January 25 1996.

9. March 2004 was a bad month for my family.

10. My sister graduated with her doctorate degree on July 3 1987.

BUILDING SKILLS 11-7: Commas with Addresses

Add commas where needed.

Example: They have moved from Los Angelesⓒ Californiaⓒ to Joplinⓒ Missouri.

1. I lived in Nashville Tennessee.

2. Send this letter to 32 S. Center Drive Scottsdale Arizona 91254.

3. Before I moved to Los Angeles California, I lived in Utah.

4. His address has been The Hilton Hotel 421 W. 13th Street Las Vegas Nevada 89501.

5. The Rowlands were married in Montgomery Alabama.

6. Bob traveled from Austin Texas to New York to attend a conference.

7. The computer show was held at the Plaza Hotel 12 Lowe Street Ontario California 85201.

8. Nathan will move to Tupelo Mississippi in January.

9. The Department of Motor Vehicles is located at 132 N. Cadillac Avenue Cypress Pennsylvania 59711.

10. My dream is to own the house on 1528 Kingsdale Drive Arlington Virginia 22202.

> ### 👆 MEMORY TIP
> There are three rules for commas that enclose:
> 1. with interrupters or scoopables
> 2. with direct address
> 3. with dates and addresses

🕯 BUILDING SKILLS TOGETHER 11-2: Commas and Writing

With a partner, read the following paragraph and add commas where needed. Do not add any other punctuation; just add commas.

(1) After I have accomplished a goal I find a way to celebrate. (2) In fact rewarding myself motivates me to accomplish more goals. (3) I reward myself by making chocolate chip cookies from scratch. (4) Two weeks ago I passed a difficult math test that had stressed me out for four days and kept me up studying for four nights. (5) I prepared well for that test by joining a study group working with a tutor and going over my notes every day. (6) Even after I completed the test I was still unsure about my performance. (7) On Tuesday the professor handed back the tests and I finally saw my excellent score. (8) Incredulous I asked the professor "Are you sure this is my test Professor?" (9) He replied "Yes Mike and good work!" (10) Impatiently I waited until class ended while thinking of my treat. (11) Finally I rushed out and bought all the ingredients for a batch of cookies. (12) My happiest moments in the kitchen were when I mixed the sticky batter licked the bowl and watched the cookies bake. (13) The cookies squares of chocolate ecstasy were a perfect gift after much misery over cramming and stressing about my math test. (14) As I enjoyed the last of my cookies I was already looking forward to accomplishing one more goal soon.

BUILDING SKILLS TOGETHER 11-3: Commas and Writing

With a partner or small group, read the following essay and add commas where needed. Do not add any other punctuation; just add commas.

(1) As Derek Johnson walked out of his World History class on Wednesday evening March 3 2010 he felt panicked. (2) The professor has just assigned a twelve-page paper due one month from today. (3) How could she? (4) Doesn't she realize how busy Derek is? (5) The syllabus has mentioned a paper but twelve pages seemed downright excessive. (6) On his way to his next class he sent a tweet from his phone complaining about it.

(7) When Derek had decided to go to college after working for a year after high school he had not realized what a juggling act it would require. (8) There was his family which included his Mom stepdad five-year-old sister and three step-brothers. (9) Then there was his full-time job an administrative assistant which was quite demanding. (10) He hoped that a degree in business would help him move into the management ranks and the higher salaries. (11) Added to all this are his other activities such as singing in his church choir coaching the youth soccer league competing in cycling races and working out every morning at the gym.

(12) His head began to swim as he thought about all his upcoming obligations like his mother's birthday next week the dog's vet appointment his stepbrother's visit and the training class he was required to attend for work. (13) Something had to go but he could not think of anything he was willing to sacrifice to make time for a twelve-page paper. (14) Still the paper was to count as 25 percent of his final grade in the course. (15) He decided he would try to think of a topic for the paper on his way home but then he remembered his mom asking him "Derek please stop at the store on your way home and pick up milk and bread." (16) Somewhere on aisle 12 between the frozen pizza and the frozen yogurt Derek's thoughts about his research paper vanished.

(17) The following week the professor asked how the papers were coming along. (18) Many of the students gave long accounts of their research progress but Derek had done nothing. (19) At the end of class three weeks later Derek saw many of the students lined up to show the professor the first drafts of their papers. (20) Derek thought to himself Derek you need to spend your

only free night of the week in the library working on this paper! (21) Sadly Derek's work session was not all that productive as he found himself obsessing about things that were bothering him at work. (22) When he glanced at his watch he was shocked to see that it was already midnight! (23) The library was closing and he had only written one page.

(24) On his way out to the car his cell rang and his Mom asked him "Derek could you watch your sister tomorrow night? She's running a fever and won't be going to school." (25) She also informed him that his boss had called about an emergency meeting at 7:00 am. (26) His twelve-page paper was due in two days! (27) In the end Derek did not turn in his research paper. (28) He had waited too long to start it and his poor time management skills destroyed his chances of success in that class.

—From Constance Staley, *Focus on College Success*

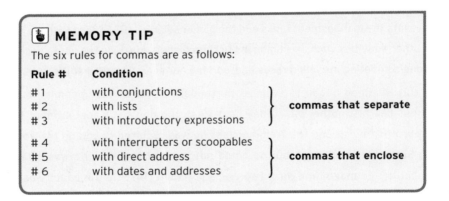

MEMORY TIP

The six rules for commas are as follows:

Rule #	Condition	
# 1	with conjunctions	
# 2	with lists	**commas that separate**
# 3	with introductory expressions	
# 4	with interrupters or scoopables	
# 5	with direct address	**commas that enclose**
# 6	with dates and addresses	

CHAPTER ELEVEN SKILLS REVIEW: Commas

Add commas where needed.

1. On my way home I saw a horrific car accident.

2. I am going to swim; then I will take a shower.

3. This criminal case however has all the elements of blackmail.

4. Nick visited Oregon Utah and Colorado.

5. The condemning decision was rendered on July 12 1989.

6. I have lived in France Italy Portugal and Greece.

7. You know Pat this is the best coffee cake I have ever tasted.

8. I love Italian food but I am tired of pizza.

9. This music group first appeared in Costa Mesa California.

10. Cynthia was born on April 10 2005.

11. By the way who was at the dinner dance last night?

12. Mary will visit her brother in Boulder Colorado; however Larry will visit his sister in Lebanon Philadelphia.

13. My boss the woman with the red hair is an amazing person.

14. Did you bring the safety lock Adam?

15. During the winter months we turn on the heaters all day.

16. Let us sign the deal tomorrow January 9 2009.

17. I must buy apples peaches bananas and pears for my fruit salad.

18. Detectives scientists who investigate cases study people's behaviors.

19. While he prepared dinner his wife set the table for six people.

20. Doctor this patient needs emergency surgery.

21. On my pizza I like the following toppings: olives mushrooms pepperoni and extra cheese.

22. Indeed he is a very confident speaker.

23. My brother Richie Luis is a famous mystery writer.

24. We arrived in Berkeley California on June 23 1986.

25. This road nevertheless should be resurfaced.

26. Mrs. Jones take some medicine for that headache before you get worse.

27. Unfortunately the concert was canceled indefinitely.

28. I chose *The Grapes of Wrath* for my book yet I have never read it.

29. Rocky's Bistro the newest restaurant in town was damaged during the earthquake.

30. This house has big windows three fireplaces and four bedrooms.

CHAPTER TWELVE: The Twelfth Building Block
Other Types of Punctuation

Some of the world's earliest written languages did not use punctuation, nor did they distinguish between uppercase and lowercase letters: they used only capital letters and spaces to show separation between words and thoughts. Over time, the English language developed a set of punctuation marks that allow readers to grasp a vast range of meanings and expressions.

When you punctuate a sentence, you add the correct punctuation marks to help clarify the meaning. Chapter Eleven focused on **comma use** in constructing clear and strong sentences. Chapter Twelve introduces six additional punctuation marks: **apostrophe, semicolon, colon, dash, hyphen,** and **quotation marks**.

APOSTROPHE '

The **apostrophe** is a mark that looks exactly like a comma but is raised and placed between letters in a word rather than between whole words. Apostrophes allow you to write more efficiently, with fewer words, in two specific situations:

1. **To show possession**

   An apostrophe allows you to take a wordy sentence like *The jacket belongs to Jim,* and to shorten it into the phrase *Jim's jacket.* Whenever you need to show that something or someone owns or possesses something or someone else, <u>always</u> use an apostrophe and <u>sometimes</u> add an -*s.* Grammar has established clear rules for how to tell when you need to add the -*s:*

   a. To show ownership with singular nouns, use the apostrophe and -*s.*

Jim's jacket	Girl's coat	Jess's hat
Everybody's turn	Anyone's question	

b. To show possession or ownership with plural nouns that do not end in —*s* or —*es*, use an apostrophe and add an -*s*.

Men's cologne   People's concern   Children's clothing

c. To show possession with plural nouns ending with -*s*, use only an apostrophe.

Girls' coats   Teams' coaches   Thomas' house

d. When two nouns are involved, apostrophes must show whether the subjects have joint or individual ownership.

My brother and sister's car (they share the same car)
My brother's and sister's cars (they each own a separate car)

e. To show possession with personal pronouns, do not use an apostrophe at all.

Yours is my favorite painting in the gallery
Whose wallet is this?

2. **To show contractions**

Contractions are effective for shortening or contracting two words into one; however, avoid using them in formal or college writing. Use an apostrophe to indicate the position of the missing letter or letters. The following verbs are often used in a contracted form:

Verbs with *not*	cannot = can't	was not = wasn't
	are not = aren't	do not = don't
Pronouns with *will*	I will = I'll	she will = she'll
	you will = you'll	they will = they'll
Pronouns and nouns with the verb *to be*	it is = it's	who is = who's
	I am = I'm	Mark is = Mark's
Pronouns with *would*	I would = I'd	we would = we'd
	he would = he'd	they would = they'd

Note: One special contraction changes letters as well as drops them: *Will not* becomes *won't* in the contracted form.

3. **To form the plurals of letters and figures.**

Cross your *t's*.   Her *p's* and *q's* all look the same.

> ### 👆 MEMORY TIP
>
> Apostrophes are required for forming contractions. Contractions save space and give the appearance that you are actually "talking" to your reader. However, in formal composition or college writing, you should avoid using contractions because of the informal tone they produce in sentences. Using the full version of a word is always grammatically correct.

BUILDING SKILLS 12-1: Using Apostrophes

Add apostrophes to the following sentences.
Example: Kyle's iPod was stolen when he was swimming.

1. The fathers car is a gorgeous blue.

2. I thought he couldnt go to the game.

3. The Johnsons cat is on the loose again.

4. His 7s are always crookedly written.

5. Everyone cheered at Bobs home run.

6. Someones umbrella has been left behind.

7. The girls lockers were broken into yesterday.

8. I wont study for my boring physics test.

9. Tesss wedding ring has been missing as of last night.

10. She always omits the *m*s when she writes.

11. Lisas sister spent last year in Bombay.

12. Have you seen Jim and Janice new mobile home?

13. It's a shame that Fred cant go on the tour.

14. I paid for Ronys concert ticket.

15. My bosss tie is expensive.

16. The couples car was towed away.

17. I quickly scribbled my notes on the folders back.

18. They were met by the hospitals attending surgeon.

19. The guitars strings needed tuning.

20. The team of doctors met to discuss the tumors treatment.

SEMICOLON ;

The **semicolon** is a punctuation mark that occupies a middle ground between the comma and the period. It tells the reader to pause longer than for a comma but to pause without the finality of a period. Semicolons are used in the following situations:

1. **To separate two independent clauses that are not already joined by a conjunction.**

   > I enjoy playing soccer; I practice for two hours every day.
   > My parents have three children; they have my twin brothers and me.

2. **To punctuate an adverbial conjunction (or HOT SHOT MAMA CAT), that follows an independent clause.**

   > ; however,   ; consequently,   ; in fact,
   > It was raining; therefore, I stayed home.

3. **To separate items in a series that already contains commas.**

   > I have lived in <u>Rome, Italy</u>; <u>Paris, France</u>; and <u>Athens, Greece</u>.

   The underlined words make up an item in the series, but each item is made up of two things: one that belongs in the other—Rome belongs inside of Italy.

   > I need to send thank-you notes to Joe, the doorman; Mrs. Katz, my neighbor who watches my cat; and Jenny, who catered the birthday party for my mother.

BUILDING SKILLS 12-2: Semicolons

Add semicolons to the following sentences.

Example: It was aimed at Harvard undergraduates(;) millions of people have become members of Facebook.

1. The teacher assigned a fun project nevertheless, the students did not want to do it.

2. Riding a motorcycle is exhilarating I do it every weekend.

3. On our vacation we went to Boston, Massachusetts Hartford, Connecticut and Detroit, Michigan.

4. The math test was hard in fact, I failed it.

5. The roads were slick from the rain many motorists lost control of their cars.

6. The Beckmans visited Amarillo, Texas Tulsa, Oklahoma Phoenix, Arizona and Reno, Nevada.

7. The price of oil has fluctuated in the past six months consequently, the stock markets have suffered.

8. Today is a beautiful day let us go play Frisbee.

9. I left the concert late however, I made it home safely.

10. The soldier's tour of duty included stops in Baghdad, Iraq Amman, Jordan and Damascus, Syria.

11. Pineapples are associated with Hawaii however, they originated in South America.

12. This computer has not been updated in two years it needs more memory.

13. Jenny ordered a parfait a dessert made of yogurt, fruit, and syrup.

14. I need to go the grocery store it is about five miles away.

15. My brother likes to watch *Start Trek*, with Captain Kirk and Mr. Spock *Star Wars*, with Luke Skywalker and Darth Vader and *Battlestar Galactica*, with its Cylons.

16. Call me tomorrow I will give you my final answer.

17. It rained heavily however, we managed to have our birthday party.

18. They have paid what they owe they should have the privileges stated in the contract.

19. We had three professors on our committee: Walter Wallace, Professor of English Mathilda Seymona, Professor of Mathematics and Anna Gill, Professor of Economics.

20. The project was complete we were glad to move on to the next one on the list.

COLON :

The **colon** is a punctuation mark used primarily to point ahead to additional information. It directs the reader to expect more and to look farther. The colon acts as an introductory device for the following kinds of information:

1. **A list that follows an independent clause**

   My favorite cars are the following: Porsches, Lamborghinis, and Bentleys.

   The independent clause that comes before a colon and a list often includes a phrase such as *the following*. A colon may only be used with an independent clause coming before it.

Incorrect: My playlist includes: Coldplay, U2, and Moby.

Correct: My playlist includes the following: Coldplay, U2, and Moby.

2. **Quotations that are formal or lengthy, or do not follow a "he said/she said" expression**

> The judge made a final, formal statement: "Based on the evidence, the jurors have one verdict that they should bring in."

Most quotations are introduced by commas, especially when the sentence includes the phrase "he said" or "she said." The colon introduces quotations that are clearly formal or especially lengthy.

3. **Explanations, questions, or titles**

> She had worked toward one goal in her life: a degree in mathematics.
> The question is: Should we surrender our troops?
> Decongestant Drugs: Their Effects on Drivers

Notice that the letter just after the colon is capitalized. Why? Either because the words that follow it make a complete sentence or because all major words in a title are capitalized.

BUILDING SKILLS 12-3: Colons

Add colons to these sentences.

Example: An essay has the following sections(:)an introduction, a body, and a conclusion.

1. The laundry list includes the following items sheets, towels, duvets and pillows.

2. My roommate is guilty of three things procrastination, fibbing, and greed.

3. That was the question To be or not to be.

4. Spirituality is like trust It cannot be forced.

5. George Orwell's famous cynicism is illustrated by this statement "Most people who bother with the matter at all would admit that the English language is in a bad way."

6. This book has won the highest most coveted award The Newbery Medal.

7. Let me repeat one point I do not tolerate tardy students.

8. I have always believed in the words of Benjamin Franklin "There never was a good war or a bad peace."

9. For the beach trip, Samantha packed only the essentials towels, sandwiches, and sunscreen.

10. I have read *The Glory of Hera Greek Mythology and the Greek Family.*

11. I used this title for my sociology paper Deviant Behavior The Link to Criminal Acts.

12. The important vitamins found in vegetables are the following vitamin A, vitamin C, thiamine, and niacin.

13. The chili recipe calls for the following items beans, tomatoes, onions, garlic, and ground beef.

14. In college, I met four friends Juan, Dakemia, Tyler, and Caroline.

15. Many people have repeated Harry Truman's classic statement "If you can't stand the heat, get out of the kitchen."

16. Nelly is taking two classes Anatomy 101 and Astronomy 240.

17. Her daughter has three things to do clean her room fold her laundry and scrub the toilets.

18. Mark Twain's humor is evident in these words "I did not have time to write a short letter, so I wrote a long one instead."

19. The ice cream comes in three flavors chocolate, vanilla, and pistachio.

20. My favorite celebrities have their own blogs Taylor Swift, Ashton Kutcher, and Jennifer Lopez.

DASH – AND PARENTHESIS ( )

The **dash** or **parenthesis** is used to signal the insertion of interrupters, or scoopables, in a sentence. Try to limit use of dashes and parentheses, especially since a pair of commas can also perform the same function for interrupters.

> ### 💡 MEMORY TIP
> Anything between two commas, dashes, or parentheses in a sentence can be removed, or scooped out, from the sentence without disturbing the basic meaning established by its subject and verb; mentally "scooping out" the words between these punctuation marks as you read or write can help you identify the subject and verb and maintain the sentence's clarity.

To use these punctuation marks effectively, you need to know their different qualities. The dash sends a stronger, more dramatic signal; parentheses are a quieter interruption to the flow of the sentence. Dashes and parentheses are used in the following specific situations:

1. **To indicate a sudden break in thought**

   It looks pretty—but did I tell you the news about the new girl?

   He is (and I'm gossiping here) a terrible cook.

2. **To insert nonessential material that adds to but does not ultimately affect the basic meaning of the sentence**

   The man—a sad sight to behold—staggered down the street.

   Waterskiing (my least favorite activity) is most popular in this area.

3. **To add emphasis or suspense**

   The shadow with the raised dagger came closer—closer.

   The squeaky noise (vibrating in the silence of the night) frazzled my nerves.

> 👆 **MEMORY TIP**
>
> A dash is typed as two hyphens with no space before or after (—).

BUILDING SKILLS 12-4: Dashes and Parentheses

Rewrite the following sentences and insert dashes and parentheses where needed.

Example: I wish you would—oh, forget it.

1. The hissing sound grew louder louder.

   _____

2. She is I am very certain not serious about her threat.

   _____

3. He said the true reason but maybe they do not care.

   _____

4. It was something said by Truman about the kitchen Was it too much heat?

   _____

5. The thumping footsteps passed the doorway and came closer closer.

   _____

6. He is I tell you an obnoxious storyteller.

   _____

7. Kevin took a few steps back, started running at full speed, kicked his leg out missed the ball.

   _____

8. Everything that went wrong from the car accident to the rude neighbor we blamed on our move.

   _____

9. In China, the basic needs of people food, clothing, and housing are less costly than in a big city like New York.

   _____

10. In the pantry, there are the main staples olive oil, rice, and beans my mother uses in her cooking.

    _____

11. Her taste in music from country to rap indicates her eclectic personality.

    _____

12. Joshua a student in my class does not have time to join the Study Abroad committee.

    _____

13. We read "Story of an Hour" Kate Chopin's short fiction in our English class.

    _____

14. Alfred Henning still singing at the age of ninety performed at the Pink Swan club.

    _____

15. Living life my way that is what I want.

    _____

16. Ideas that is opinions backed with sound reasoning are hard to develop in an essay.

    _____

17. The nutritional value if the term can be applied to licorice is minimal.

    _____

18. All four of them Harry Henry Hal and Howie did well in school.

    _____

19. Never have I met such a nice person before you.

    _____

20. Please call my hardworking agent Jennifer Polopa about hiring me for that movie role.

    _____

HYPHEN -

The **hyphen**—which is a shorter mark than the dash—is used to bring two or more standard English words (i.e., found in the dictionary) together into a compound word.

twenty-four   mother-in-law   mid-July

The use of hyphens is a matter of changing style. A current dictionary should always be consulted when you have a question about whether or not to hyphenate a compound word. If the compound word is not in the dictionary, treat it as two words.

BUILDING SKILLS 12-5: Hyphens

Rewrite the following sentences and insert hyphens where needed.
Example: We got stuck on a one(-)way street.

1. I bought a water repellant snowsuit.

2. She is not a well known politician and she is in her mid forties.

3. One third of my income pays for medical care, and one fifth pays the rent.

4. Mr. Grasso has bought seven self help books to read in the next month.

5. Alicia hated the movie; it reminded her of her abusive father in law.

6. The under prepared workers felt overwhelmed by the amount of work.

7. The hand carved wood box attracted the attention of many customers.

8. I hope Daniella Smythe will be re elected to Senate.

9. He changed that minor mistake on the spot.

10. My grandmother advocates kindness to all four legged friends.

11. A long awaited verdict was finally reached.

———————————————————————————————

12. His second ex wife sued for alimony.

———————————————————————————————

13. Bryan's easy going nature causes others to underestimate him.

———————————————————————————————

14. My youngest child is a happy go lucky person.

———————————————————————————————

15. Her fifteen minute tirade demonstrated her anger at the protestors.

———————————————————————————————

16. They planned to get married in mid July when the weather turned warmer.

———————————————————————————————

17. The kindergarten teacher had thirty six children in her class.

———————————————————————————————

18. He acquired a semi permanent living arrangement at the new senior citizens center.

———————————————————————————————

19. They re emphasized the importance of horse vaccinations due to the West Nile virus.

———————————————————————————————

20. It is a well known fact that he is a self made millionaire.

———————————————————————————————

QUOTATION MARKS " "

Quotation marks are used to identify a person's exact speech or thoughts, as well as to label different types of titles and words. There are specific grammar rules for presenting quotation marks in various situations:

1. **Use double quotation marks to set off <u>direct quotations.</u>**
   Direct quotations repeat the exact words (verbatim) of someone's speech or from written documents. **Double quotation marks** are used to set off direct quotations and are often presented with conversational words or words that signal dialogue, speech, or written words, such as *said, wrote, explained, asked, maintained, insisted,* etc.

   > Charles Dickens said, "It was the best of times; it was the worst of times."
   > "Why didn't you wait for me?" Ahmet cried. "I came as quickly as I could!"

When using quotation marks with direct quotations, there are specific rules for punctuation:

a. **Before a quotation:** Place a comma or colon <u>after</u> the conversational word and open the quotation marks.

> . . . said, "He is a good person."

b. **At the end of a quotation**: Periods and commas are always placed <u>inside</u> the ending quotation mark.

> "Talk to Michael."
> "Imagine all these waiting people,"

c. **Semicolons and colons** are placed <u>outside</u> the ending quotation mark.

d. **Question marks and exclamation points** are placed <u>outside</u> the ending quotation mark, except when the quotation itself is a question or exclamation.

> Did Lisa say, "Anyone for a swim"?
> Lisa asked, "Anyone for a swim?"

e. **When the directly quoted material is split into several parts, the punctuation differs slightly.**

> "Come on Bella," Mary said. "Let's go see if Phil won this game."

f. **Single quotation marks (' ') are used to set off a quotation within a direct quotation.**

> Timothy said, "Don't you remember what she said? She said, 'All the world is looking at us.' "

2. **Use double quotation marks to set off <u>titles</u>.** Titles of shorter pieces of writing such as magazine articles, essays, short stories or poems, chapters in books, or pieces of writing published as part of a larger work all use quotation marks around them.

> Have you read "A Good Man is Hard To Find," a short story by Flannery O'Connor?
> My favorite Beatles song is "Let it Be."

3. **Use double quotation marks to set off <u>slang, technical terms, or special words</u>.**

> In their communications, American teens use the words "Da Bomb" to mean something is wonderful or awesome. (Slang)

"Googling" and "Facebooking" are two new verbs that have recently entered the English language. (Technical term)
There are many rock and roll icons, but Elvis is the only true "King." (Special word)

 MEMORY TIP

Be careful about confusing direct quotations with indirect quotations. An indirect quotation is a reporting of what someone said without using the exact words. It does not have any quotation marks and is indicated by the word *that*.

Indirect Quotation: Mario said that he prefers the pizza to the spaghetti.

Direct Quotation: Mario said, "I prefer the pizza to the spaghetti."

BUILDING SKILLS 12-6: Direct Quotation Marks

Punctuate and complete the following sentences, including all necessary quotation marks.

Example: Mr. Dramer, who was working in the wheat field, said, "The alien spaceship landed right before my own two eyes."

1. He asked Have you ever been. . .

_____

_____

2. We are having a quiz today said Mrs. Marques Be sure to. . .

_____

_____

3. The captain said When the ship was docked the man who came aboard told me I never thought I would ever. . .

_____

_____

4. My friend's favorite Beatles song is. . .

_____

_____

5. She asked What is the price of. . .

_____

_____

6. Our teacher declared The homework is. . .

_____

_____

7. May I borrow your book asked Mary I need to. . .

_____

_____

8. Did you see the article titled Cyber Bullying in the. . .

_____

_____

9. The Center for Disease Control announced that the H1N1 Virus has been. . .

_____

_____

10. The word Fave is used by American teens to mean. . .

_____

_____

BUILDING SKILLS 12-7: Indirect Quotations

Determine which of these sentences are indirect quotations and write _Indirect_ on the line.

Example: <u>Indirect</u> Mr. Dramer, who was working in the wheat field, reported that an alien spaceship landed right before his eyes.

_____ 1. Mother said that the weather will be cold today.

_____ 2. The man asked, "How do I get to E Street?"

_____ 3. I said that I had watched that movie.

_____ 4. Maury stated that the bridge is not safe to cross.

_____ 5. May commented, "That treasure map is an interesting find."

_____ 6. Mr. Davidson warned, "We must finish this document by midnight tonight."

_____ 7. They declared that today will be a national holiday.

_____ 8. Father said that dinner is ready.

_____ 9. Professor Talley declared, "Clear your desks and get ready for a quiz."

_____ 10. I am not sure she said that she is visiting today.

🕯 BUILDING SKILLS TOGETHER 12-1: Other Types of Punctuation and Writing

In a small group, read the essay carefully and edit for punctuation errors. Periods are provided for ease of reading.

Hooked on Facebook

(1) Imagine a drug that would make American teenagers think and talk more about the timeless concerns of adolescence Whos cool whos cute and whos going out with whom. (2) Then imagine that millions of teens were taking this drug every day. (3) Actually you dont have to. (4) The drug already exists and its called MySpace. (5) There's a competitor drug known as Facebook. (6) Between one half and three quarters of American teens already have a profile on an Internet social networking site where they spend hours per week nobody really knows how many sharing pictures gossip and jokes. (7) We should all be worried about this although not for the reasons you might suspect.

(8) The newspapers keep reminding us about online predators on the Net which makes us miss the digital forest for the trees. (9) In this medium the real danger doesnt come from depraved adults. (10) It s much subtler than that and it comes from teenagers themselves specifically from their insatiable desire to hang out with each other. (11) And the key word here is insatiable.

(12) Teens have always wanted to hang out with each other. (13) But the Internet lets them do it 24/7 transforming the social world of adolescence into an omnipresence. (14) Last years report by the MacArthur Foundation on digital youth confirmed that most teens communicate online with kids they already know and theyre doing it more than ever. (15) The report states Young people use new media to build friendships and romantic relationships as well as to hang out with each other as much and as often as possible. Teenagers would say duh and they would ask What's the problem with that (16) Nothing really

except for what it replaces solitude. Once youre always on as the kids describe you're never alone. (17) That means youre less likely to read a book for pleasure to draw a picture or simply to stare out the window and imagine worlds other than your own. (18) And as any parent with a teen could testify youre less likely to communicate with the real people in your immediate surroundings. (19) Who wants to talk to family members when friends are just a click away?

(20) While many teens communicate with strangers on the Net they are also adept at sniffing out creepy adults whose threats have been vastly overblown by media reports. (21) Consider all the ink spilled over Lori Drew the Missouri woman who used a phony MySpace account to trick a teenager into believing that Drew was a male suitor. (22) When the fake suitor dumped the teen and she committed suicide you would have thought every kid in America was somehow in danger. (23) Theyre not at least not from strangers. (24) According to the Pew Research Center 32 percent of American teens say they have been contacted on the Net by someone they don t know but just 7 percent report feeling scared and uncomfortable as a result.

(25) When teens do feel hurt by something on the Internet it usually comes from surprise other adolescents at their schools. (26) About one third of teenagers say they have been the target of online bullying such as threatening messages or embarrassing pictures. (27) But two thirds of teens say bullying is more likely to happen offline than online. (28) The Internet just makes it easier to do and harder to escape.

(29) So what should todays adults do in the face of this new challenge? (30) We can try to limit our teenagers computer time of course but thats probably a lost cause by now. (31) The better solution as always comes from the kids themselves. (32) Teens around the country have started a small online movement against social networking sites trying to make them seem uncool. (33) My best friend's daughter just took down her Facebook page for example insisting that the site was for losers. (34) So pass the word to every teen you know social networking is for losers. (35) Just don't tell them I said so.

–From Jonathan Zimmerman, *"Hooked on Facebook."* San Francisco Chronicle, March 30, 2009, p. A19.
Copyright © 2009 by The San Francisco Chronicle. Reprinted by permission.

CHAPTER TWELVE SKILLS REVIEW: Punctuation

Add the necessary punctuation marks to the following sentences. You may need to add apostrophes, semicolons, colons, dashes, hyphens, and/or quotation marks. You may have to rewrite some of the sentences on the line provided.

1. Our club has these three members Candy, Brandy, and Lori.

   _____

   _____

2. My son always forgets to cross his ts and dot his *is*.

   _____

   _____

3. The question must be boldly stated Where do we go from here?

   _____

   _____

4. I cannot go with you she said I need time to heal from the heartbreak.

   _____

   _____

5. Their house has been standing tall for the last forty five years.

   _____

   _____

6. I completed my assignment I even turned it in early.

   _____

   _____

7. The detective found the following clues a broken lock, a stain of blood on the carpet, and a forgotten glove.

   _____

   _____

8. The document Working Words is finally finished.

   _____

   _____

9. She wont change her mind about not coming with me.

---

10. He has lived in Boise, Idaho Tacoma, Washington and Portland, Oregon.

---

11. I titled my essay Stem Cell Research Adopt It.

---

12. My mom said that the next door neighbor is incredibly rude.

---

13. He came to tell her that he is leaving however, she was not home.

---

14. The boys hats hang by the door.

---

15. Tucker said Don't forget that Dad said Nice people finish last.

---

16. Let's play a game of cards he suggested.

---

17. Two sisters Mary and Dalia called him Dad.

---

18. She is my crazy sister in law.

---

19. You the egotistic one must stop stealing time from all the others!

    _____

    _____

20. Thomas said They will come back for us like they said We never forget our own

    _____

    _____

APPENDIX A: Parts of Speech

Every word you write or speak falls into one of seven categories or kinds. These are collectively called the parts of speech. The seven parts of speech are nouns, pronouns, verbs, adjectives, adverbs, prepositions, conjunctions, and interjections.

NOUNS

Nouns are words that name a person, place, things, or ideas. Often, nouns are preceded by article adjectives such as *the, a, an.*

> The dog
> A girl
> An ant
>
> The <u>sky</u> is blue.
> <u>Hurricanes</u> terrify me.
> Their <u>belief</u> in the <u>right</u> of all <u>human beings</u> to live in peace is what motivates the protestors.

PRONOUNS

Pronouns are words used to take the place of nouns, either to allow the writer to refer back to the noun without repeating it each time, or to allow the writer to refer to something or someone that is not specifically identified.

Manny calls Manny's teacher to tell the teacher that Manny will be late.
Manny calls <u>his</u> teacher to tell <u>her</u> that <u>he</u> will be late.

<u>Something</u> is bothering me.
Why didn't you tell <u>anyone</u>?

The noun that a pronoun replaces is called the **antecedent**. Pronouns that refer to a <u>clearly identified</u> antecedent are called **definite pronouns**.

I, me, my, myself
he, him, his, himself
she, her, hers, herself
it, its, itself
they, them, their, themselves
you, your, yourselves
we, us, our, ours, ourselves
who, whose, which, what
that, this, these, those

Pronouns that refer to a noun that is <u>not clearly identified</u> are called **indefinite pronouns.**

anybody	nobody	somebody	everybody
anything	nothing	something	everything
Anyone	no one	someone	everyone
each	either	neither	

<u>I</u> talk to <u>him</u>.
<u>This</u> is my wallet.
<u>Everyone</u> is here.
<u>He</u> likes to talk to <u>himself</u>.

VERBS
Verbs are words that show action or show a state of being.
   Action verbs: *play, eat, talk, jump,* and *dance.*

I <u>walk</u> home.

Being verbs: the verb *to be: is, am, are, was, were, will be.*

I <u>am</u> a mother.
He <u>is</u> a monster.

Helping verbs come before the main verb to refine and clarify the exact nature and timing of the action: *is, was, were, has, have, had, will have, will be.*

He <u>is going</u> to the mall.
We <u>had helped</u> every time.
It <u>will be raining</u> soon.

Verbs that show actions taking place in a specific time (past, present, future) change their forms according to which time, or tense, is indicated. Verbs describing actions that are theoretical, or outside of a specific time, take a form called infinitive. Tenses are described in detail on pages 29–44.

ADJECTIVES

Adjectives are words that modify nouns or pronouns in a sentence, and they often fall in front of the noun or pronoun. They answer the questions: *Which one? What kind?* and *How many?* Adjectives include small **articles** like *the* and *a.*

<u>The red</u> car
<u>The noisy</u> river
<u>Three</u> birds

ADVERBS

Adverbs are words that modify the verb, adjectives, and other adverbs, and they answer the questions: *How? Where? When?* and *To what degree?*

He answered <u>quickly</u>.
They flew <u>south</u>.
The ship sailed <u>last week</u>.
She was <u>somewhat</u> angry.

PREPOSITIONS

Prepositions are words that help signal a place (*above, inside, behind*), time (*before, after, within*), or source (*to, from, for, of, by*). Consult the list below for more prepositions:

Place		Time	Source	
above	across	after	about	against
among	around	before	at	by
below	behind	during	because of	due to
beneath	beside	until	except	for
between	beyond	since	from	of
by	in/into		off	to
inside	near		toward	with
out	outside		without	here
over	on			
through	under			
up	upon			
within				

CONJUNCTIONS

Conjunctions are words that join two or more words, phrases, or clauses with one another. There are three kinds of conjunctions: coordinating, subordinating, and adverbial.

Coordinating conjunctions tell the reader that the independent clauses being joined are equal or similar in importance. An acronym you may consider using to remember the coordinating conjunctions is FANBOYS.

> The day turned out to be cloudy <u>yet</u> warm.
>
> I like milk, <u>but</u> I prefer hot chocolate with breakfast.
>
> Do you want sugar <u>or</u> milk in your coffee?

<u>Coordinating conjunctions or FANBOYS</u>

F	for	(meaning "because" or "since")
A	and	(meaning "in addition")
N	nor	(meaning "and neither")
B	but	(meaning "on the contrary" or "however")
O	or	(meaning "alternatively")
Y	yet	(meaning "even" "however" or "but")
S	so	(meaning "therefore")

Adverbial conjunctions link independent clauses. These clauses must be separated by an adverbial conjunction and punctuated with a semicolon before the conjunction and a comma behind it. An acronym you may consider using to remember the adverbial conjunctions is HOT SHOT MAMA CAT.

He was finished; <u>therefore,</u> he went home.

<u>Adverbial conjunctions or HOT SHOT MAMA CAT</u>

H	; **h**owever,	(meaning "but")
O	; **o**therwise,	(meaning "if not" "or else")
T	; **t**herefore,	(meaning "for that reason")
S	; **s**imilarly,	(meaning "likewise")
H	; **h**ence,	(meaning "for that reason")
O	; **o**n the other hand,	(meaning "in contrast")
T	; **t**hus,	(meaning "so" or "in this way")
M	; **m**eanwhile,	(meaning "while")
A	; **a**dditionally,	(meaning "also")
M	; **m**oreover,	(meaning "in addition")
A	; **a**lso,	(meaning "in addition")
C	; **c**onsequently,	(meaning "so")
A	; **a**s a matter of fact,	(meaning "in fact")
T	; **t**hen,	(meaning "next" or "so")

More Adverbial Conjunctions			
; in addition,	; besides,	; furthermore,	; for instance,
; instead,	; for example,	; nevertheless,	; nonetheless,
; indeed,	; likewise,	; in fact,	

Subordinating conjunctions join independent and dependent clauses. (See pp. 000–000 for more on dependent clauses.) An acronym you may consider using to remember the most common subordinating conjunctions is WASBIT.

I like my job <u>though</u> I am not satisfied with the salary.
<u>Although</u> she is in pain, she is not letting it show.

Subordinating conjunctions or WASBIT

W	**W**hen, **W**here, **W**herever, **W**henever, **W**hereas, **W**hether, **W**hile
A	**A**s, **A**s if, **A**s long as, **A**s though, **A**lthough
S	**S**ince, **S**o that
B	**B**efore, **B**ecause
I	**I**f
T	**T**hough

Other Subordinating Conjunctions		
even though	rather than	until
provided that	once	unless

INTERJECTIONS

Interjections are words that show surprise or emotion.

Oh, I do not like it.

When an interjection appears alone, it is usually followed with an exclamation mark.

Wow!   **Cowabunga!**   **Finally!**

APPENDIX A SKILLS REVIEW: Identifying Parts of Speech

In the space provided next to each sentence, identify the part of speech of each underlined word or group of words.

N	noun	Adj	adjective	Conj	conjunction
Pro	pronoun	Adv	adverb	Inter	interjection
V	verb	Prep	preposition		

1. The <u>cat</u> ran <u>under</u> the porch.   _____   _____

2. <u>It</u> is a <u>hairy</u> creature with a bad smell.   _____   _____

3. During the <u>storm,</u> <u>we</u> hid under the bed.   _____   _____

4. <u>Finally,</u> the rain <u>is</u> here.   _____   _____

5. I like dogs, <u>but</u> I <u>prefer</u> cats.   _____   _____

6. Many <u>are</u> interested in <u>conspiracy</u> theories.   _____ _____

7. <u>Everyone</u> <u>had</u> to go home because of the storm.   _____ _____

8. He speaks <u>clearly</u> and <u>eloquently</u>.   _____ _____

9. The mayor of the town <u>is hiding</u> <u>something</u>
   from the people.   _____ _____

10. <u>When</u> Tim returns, <u>we</u> will go to the movies.   _____ _____

11. The <u>red</u> corvette <u>spun</u> its wheels.   _____ _____

12. After a <u>brief</u> marriage, Jay's wife left <u>him</u>.   _____ _____

13. <u>Respect</u> is <u>easily</u> given in many relationships.   _____ _____

14. The lion ate <u>hungrily</u> as the people <u>watched</u> him.   _____ _____

15. The <u>famous</u> threesome, Larry, Moe, and Curley, <u>were</u> the   _____ _____
    Three Stooges.

16. Japan has a <u>long</u> history of protest against nuclear <u>power</u>.   _____ _____

17. <u>You</u> cannot make a dish like spinach soufflé rise <u>quickly</u>. _____ _____

18. His <u>forced</u> smile and <u>jovial</u> manner are misleading.   _____ _____

19. He was a muddled, <u>irrational</u> man <u>with</u> a mean streak.   _____ _____

20. <u>Someone</u> <u>carefully</u> picked up the injured bird.   _____ _____

21. He seems to be a tyrant, <u>and</u> I know
    he <u>will hurt</u> someone.   _____ _____

22. She is a good speaker; <u>however,</u> I did not
    like <u>her</u> message.   _____ _____

23. <u>Inside</u> the house <u>was</u> a huge mess of debris.   _____ _____

24. Jim argues <u>intelligently</u> and <u>confidently</u>.   _____ _____

25. This <u>woman</u> is deprived of any sense, <u>and</u> she is
    short on looks.   _____ _____

26. <u>His</u> mind is a <u>howling</u> wilderness.   _____ _____

27. We walked <u>behind</u> the officer <u>silently</u>.   _____ _____

28. <u>Over</u> the ocean, a <u>dark</u> storm is forming.   _____ _____

29. <u>Since</u> you are here, you can <u>help</u> me with dinner.   _____ _____

30. <u>Oh</u>, the president just walked <u>in</u>!   _____ _____

APPENDIX B: Spelling

Spelling errors are easy for readers to spot. Even if you are a weak speller, you may find yourself noticing spelling errors in e-mails, business documents, website articles, and other written texts. Anytime your brain notices an error in the writing, your flow of thought is interrupted, and your brain must back up and start over. In this way, misspellings and grammar errors detract from good writing and create bad impressions.

Computer companies have tried to help writers avoid spelling errors by inventing the handy "spell check" button. Spell Check will swiftly highlight any misspelled words; however, it judges each word in the document in isolation rather than in the context of a whole sentence. Words that *seem* to be spelled right but are actually errors will usually be missed by Spell Check. For example, the word *from* is sometimes misspelled as *form;* Spell Check will not pick up on the difference in meaning and will not point it out as a mistake. Likewise, *to, too,* and *two* are all spelled correctly but commonly misused. Your efforts to improve your own "spell check" abilities, therefore, will pay off in stronger, smoother writing. To become a better speller, always proofread your writing.

Proofreading is checking a piece of writing for accuracy and correctness. Its purpose is to catch any careless mistakes that might distract or confuse readers. Proofreading is best done *after* all substantial changes, improvements, and additions have been made to a piece of writing.

The key to proofreading is to see what is actually on the page rather than what you intended to put on the page. You need to find ways to see the text with fresh eyes. Try the following techniques:

- Print out your writing and proofread on hard copy.
- Read your paper aloud.

- Ask someone else to read your paper aloud, and listen carefully as he or she reads.
- Run your writing through a spell-check program.
- Read your text backward. Turn to the last line of your paper, hold a ruler or pencil over the line just above, and move it up as you read from the bottom up, checking one word at a time.

CREATE SPELLING LISTS

Create a list of words you have trouble with and update the list as you encounter new words. Check to see whether a word that you find troublesome shares a root, prefix, or suffix with a word you already know; the connection helps you learn the meaning, as well as the spelling, of the new word.

LEARN THE *EI/IE* RULE

Write *i* before *e* except after *c* (or when it sounds like *a* as in *neighbor* or *weigh*).

i **before *e*:**	chief	piece	brief	yield	priest
after *c*:	ceiling	receive	receipt	perceive	deceive
sounds like *a*:	eight	freight	vein	their	neighbor

Note: Four exceptions exist to this rule: *Leisure, seizure, foreign,* and *height* all have *ei* spellings, though none of the four come after *c* or sound like *a*.

BUILDING SKILLS APPENDIX B-1: Writing *ie* or *ei*

Circle the correct spelling of each word.

1. field   feild
2. reciept   receipt
3. deciet   deceit
4. achieve   acheive
5. hieght   height

KNOW COMMONLY MISSPELLED WORDS

Many words are misspelled because of their unusual letter combinations or incorrect pronunciation.

Incorrect	Correct
sincerly	sincerely
fourty	forty
libary	library
payed	paid
judgement	judgment
coperate	cooperate
goverment	government
seperate	separate
necesary	necessary
privaledge	privilege

BUILDING SKILLS APPENDIX B-2: Misspelled Words

Underline the misspelled words in the following paragraph and write the correct spelling on the numbered lines. There are 17 spelling errors.

(1) There is a need to protect the animals and the envirment. (2) In Africa, consrvachionists are concerned about the perservattion of elephants because it is necesary to protect this magnificent animal. (3) Ever since the sale of ivory has been banned by international lawmakers, illegal hunting of elephants has declined. (4) Therfore, the number of elephants has increased as has the number of cities and metropolitans. (5) This endengrs the elephants' habitat and makes them competors for space with farmers who live around thier areas. (6) As a result, African farmers often complain to the goverments that elephants have ruined their crops. (7) This creates a situation for despirate measures and technics such as lighting fires, chili-coating fences, or gun shooting to stop elephants form coming onto their feilds. (8) The occurances of violence are escalating causing conservationists to develop clever strategies to protect the elephant popolation because in the end, humans are priviledged to share the elephants' habitat.

1. _____   7. _____

2. _____   8. _____

3. _____   9. _____

4. _____   10. _____

5. _____   11. _____

6. _____   12. _____

13. _____   16. _____

14. _____   17. _____

15. _____

KNOW COMMONLY CONFUSED WORDS

Words that sound alike or look alike can cause frequent spelling errors. Here's a list of confusing pairs of words. You may want to copy out portions of this list into your own journal. The act of physically writing out the different spellings of each pair will help you learn to distinguish between them.

Accept: to receive (verb)   I accept your decision.
Except: other than (preposition)   I greeted everyone except you.

Advice: guidance (noun)   I like your advice.
Advise to give guidance (verb)   She advised me to drop the class.

Affect: to influence (verb)   The pollution affects our lungs.
Effect: result (noun)   Pollution has a strong effect on our lungs.

All ready: all (pronoun) are   The passengers were all ready to board
   ready (adverb)   the ship.
Already: before (adverb)   I did this assignment already.

Brake: to stop (verb)   The train brakes at railroad signs.
Break: to come apart (verb)   That vase breaks easily.

Capital: city or money (noun)   He raised capital for his business venture.
                       Sacramento is the capital of California.
Capitol: a building (noun)   Washington has a capitol building.

Clothes: apparel (noun)   I wear my clothes.
Cloths: fabric (plural noun)   My clothes are made from cloths.

Conscience: moral guide (noun)   Lies are against my conscience.
Conscious: awake or aware (adverb)   The accident victim was not conscious.

Desert: dry land (noun)   The desert climate is hot.
Dessert: sweet food (noun)   Apple pie is a great dessert.

Heard: past tense of *to hear* (verb) I heard a rumor about the war.
Herd: a group of animals (noun)   The herd of cows is let out.

Its: shows possession (pronoun)   The cat ate its food.
It's: a contraction of *It* and *is* It's a good day.

Knew: past tense of *to know* (verb)   I knew a sweet man.
New: recent, not old (adjective)   My new boots squeak.

Loose: not too tight (adjective)   My pants are loose on my waist.
Lose: not to win (verb)   I always lose at Scrabble.

Personal: private (adjective)   This is a personal matter.
Personnel: employees (plural noun)   The personnel at the company are frustrated.

Principal: leader (noun)   She is the principal of our school.
Principle: rule or concept (noun)   America is based on the principle of democracy.

Quite: entirely or very (adverb)   The dress is quite lovely.
Quiet: silent (adjective)   He is a quiet person.
Quit: to stop (verb)   I quit my job.

Then: next in time (adverb)   We danced then ate.
Than: to compare (conjunction)   He is shorter than Doris.

Their: shows possession (pronoun)   This is their house.
There: indicates location (preposition)   There is my iPhone.
They're: a contraction of *they* and *are*   They're my students.

Thought: past tense of *to think* (verb)   I thought of him always.
Though: form of *although* (conjunction)   Though he is gone, I still love him.

Weather: climate (noun)   The weather is cold.
Whether: either or in case (conjunction)   We should know whether it will rain tonight.

BUILDING SKILLS APPENDIX B-3: Commonly Confused Words

Circle the right word choice for each sentence.

1. Sanford will (accept, except) his award at the ceremony.

2. Is everyone (all ready, already) to go on the picnic?

3. We will solve this problem (then, than) watch a movie.

4. I am (quit, quiet, quite) happy with the new arrangement.

5. Will you follow her (advice, advise)?

6. This restaurant offers the sweetest chocolate (dessert, desert).

7. The class will have (its, it's) final exam today.

8. That dress is (lose, loose) on me now.

9. I (thought, though) things through, and I have made a decision.

10. The students finished (their, there, they're) projects.)

11. I (knew, new) that this was not appropriate conduct.

12. This a matter of (personal, personnel) importance.

13. Mrs. Burke is the (principal, principle) at the Saint Dorothy School.

14. He wants to (quit, quiet, quite) his job.

15. He does not know (whether, weather) to jump for joy or cry.

16. (Their, There, They're) is an error with this chemistry problem.

17. The counselor (advised, adviced) me about the best course of action.

18. Farmers must have a (heard, herd) of cattle to survive.

19. I always pump the (brake, break) when I am skidding on icy roads.

20. The (desert, dessert) is not a safe place for children.

21. We need more (capital, capitol) for our business expansion.

22. I follow the (principle, principal) of equality and fairness.

23. The (cloths, clothes) that my (cloths, clothes) are made of are expensive.

24. We have (all ready, already) packed the van for the trip.

25. The Brown family lives on a (quiet, quit, quite) street.

26. I always (lose, loose) my car keys.

27. My (conscience, conscious) will not allow me to lie to anyone.

28. Do you think (its, it's) too late to register for classes?

29. She (heard, herd) the bad rumor about their breakup.

30. The (effect, affect) of the budget cuts is massive.

KNOW WORD ENDINGS

Sometimes, the spelling error occurs in how we spell the *end* of a word. This occurs most commonly when we are changing a word from the singular to the plural form. Here are a few guidelines to keep in mind:

1. For words ending in *s, ss, x, z, sh,* or *ch* add an *–es*

   boxes   churches   mistresses   fizzes   dishes

2. For words ending in *f* or *fe*, change the *f* to *y* and add *–es*

   shelf   shelves   wife   wives

3. For words ending in *o* preceded by a **vowel** (*a,e,i,o,u*) add *–s*. For words ending in *o* preceded by a **consonant,** add *–es*

with vowels:	zoo	zoos	rodeo	rodeos
with consonant:	hero	heroes	tomato	tomatoes

4. For words ending in *y*, change the y to *i* and add *–es*

   city   cities   lily   lilies   candy   candies

5. For some words, no ending is required to show the plural form

   fish   sheep   series   deer

6. For some words, we change the whole word, not just the ending

   child   children   man   men   tooth   teeth

7. For Greek and Latin nouns, there are special spellings to show plural form:

datum	data	thesis	theses	criterion
syllabus	syllabi	analysis	analyses	criteria

BUILDING SKILLS APPENDIX B-6: Word Endings

Write the correct plural form for each noun.

1. life   _____

2. spoon   _____

3. woman   _____

4. half   _____

5. story   _____

6. studio   _____

7. miss   _____

8. fox   _____

9. radio   _____

10. zero   _____

11. chief   _____

12. echo   _____

13. wolf   _____

14. baby   _____

15. mouse   _____

16. fish   _____

17. roof   _____

18. puppy   _____

19. crisis   _____

APPENDIX B SKILLS REVIEW: Spelling

Correct any spelling errors in the following sentences by crossing out the incorrectly spelled word and writing the correct spelling above it.

1. Jim's neice did not like studying too much.

2. Kacey likes potatos, but she does not except them baked, only freid.

3. I could not beleive that she had pasted away.

4. Their are many judgements against this lose criminal.

5. Mr. Martin believes a man is happiest married to many wifes.

6. My father always said, "lilys only grow in the valleys."

7. My brother's friends enjoy hunting for there deers.

8. Our twin childs are about to start college.

9. The analysises of the scientists revealed that extintions of dinosaurs probally ocured from a meteor strike.

10. My favourite contractor repairs and installs rooves.

11. I misplaced the reciept for my grocery purchases.

12. Admiting to misstakes is better than dennying them.

13. I do not quit understand why it is so quite.

14. I ordered iegth peices of chicken for my complementory meal.

15. He should have apoligized sincerly to the womans.

APPENDIX C: English as a Second Language Concerns

If you have a language other than English as your first language, you may need some extra help with certain areas of grammar. You may have realized that no two languages have the same grammar, and that the English language—more than many other language—has a confusing set of rules with many exceptions. This section gathers some of these exceptions in one place, so you can focus on learning them quickly and well.

NOUNS

Nouns are words that name a place, person, or thing. Examples include: cat, teacher, mountain, or city.

Nouns come in two categories:
1. **Count nouns** are nouns that can be counted.

   The table is old.

   The noun in this sentence is specific because it names an individual item that can be counted, touched, or seen or handled— table.

2. **Noncount nouns** are nouns that cannot be counted. Most noncount nouns suggest a group of things or an abstract idea.

   The furniture is old.

   The noun in this sentence is not specific because it names a general category. Furniture is a group that can include many tables or many different pieces to make up what we call furniture.

In short, count nouns name specific things, places, or people, whereas noncount nouns name general things, places, or people.

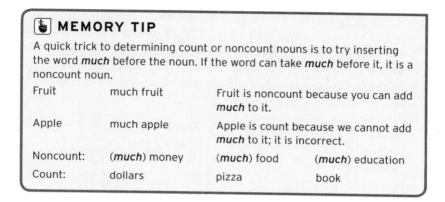

> ### 👆 MEMORY TIP
> A quick trick to determining count or noncount nouns is to try inserting the word *much* before the noun. If the word can take *much* before it, it is a noncount noun.
>
> | Fruit | much fruit | Fruit is noncount because you can add *much* to it. |
> |---|---|---|
> | Apple | much apple | Apple is count because we cannot add *much* to it; it is incorrect. |
>
> | Noncount: | (*much*) money | (*much*) food | (*much*) education |
> |---|---|---|---|
> | Count: | dollars | pizza | book |

ARTICLES

Many nouns in English require a part of speech called an **article** to introduce them in a sentence. There are only three articles—*a, an,* and *the*—and they appear always and only before nouns.

Can you bring me <u>a</u> glass of water?

Before <u>an</u> exam, I always feel nervous.

<u>The</u> storm in <u>the</u> night flooded our street.

How do you decide which article to use with a given noun? Learning to ask and answer two questions will lead you to a correct decision: First, is the noun **definite** or **indefinite**? Second, is the sound that begins the noun a **vowel** or a **consonant**?

1. **Definite or indefinite?** Nouns that are specific, designated, exact, identified, or known take the **definite article** *the*.

No, not this one; I need <u>the book</u> with <u>the blue cover.</u>

The article *the* tells the reader that the noun which follows it is exact, identified, specific, and known. Not just any book, cat, country, idea—a definite one. In contrast, the article *a* tells the reader that the noun which follows it is unspecified, general, abstract, vague, or unidentified. *A* and *an,* therefore, are **indefinite articles.**

Oh, <u>a book</u> with any cover—red, blue, black—will be fine.

2. **Does the noun begin with a vowel or consonant sound?** This question does not apply to the definite article *the*. Once you determine that the noun will take a definite article, you have only one choice: *the*. Indefinite articles, however, offer two choices: *a* and *an*. What's the difference? There is no difference between them except spelling: the "n" is simply added when the noun begins with a vowel sound, in order to make it easier to pronounce. Try saying "a apple," then say "an apple." Which phrase is easier to produce with your tongue? Vowel sounds are *a, e, i, o,* and *u*. Consonant sounds are any letter in the alphabet EXCEPT for *a, e, i, o, u*:

> I need <u>an</u> envelope.   That is <u>an</u> insult!
>
> I need <u>a</u> recipe for cookies.   That's <u>a</u> great car!

VERBS

In several languages, verbs are nonexistent, but in English, **verbs** tell what action the subject in a sentence performs. Verbs also tell the time of the action.

There are twelve different tenses of verbs, and each one refers to a time when the action happened. Refer back to Chapter Two for complete explanations, examples, and exercises on verbs.

For non-native speakers or speakers of nonstandard English, the most confusing aspects of verbs are:

1. **The use of helping verbs** such as: *has, have, had, will have, is, am, are, was, were, will be, have been, has been,* or *had been*.

> Incorrect: It snow all day yesterday.
>
> Correct: It <u>had snowed</u> all day yesterday.
>
> It <u>had been snowing</u> all day yesterday.

2. **The –*ing* verbs**: these verbs always require the verb *to be* as a helping verb.

> Incorrect: I going to the mall.
>
> Correct: I <u>am going</u> to the mall.
>
> I <u>was going</u> to the mall.

PREPOSITIONS

A **preposition** is a part of speech which is used to indicate place, time, or source. Here are some of the many prepositions in the English language:

Place		Time	Source	
above	across	after	about	against
among	around	before	at	by
below	behind	during	because of	due to
beneath	beside	until	except	for
between	beyond	since	from	of
by	in/into		off	to
inside	near		toward	with
out	outside		without	
over	on			
through	under			
up	upon			
within				

Prepositions can be tricky to identify, because they can be used as adjectives, adverbs, or prepositions. A true preposition will always be paired with an object.

Preposition with object: **Martha looked <u>up the phone number.</u>**
Not used as preposition: **Martha looked <u>up</u>.**
Preposition with object: **We scraped the paint <u>off the table</u>.**
Not used as preposition: **The computer turned <u>off</u>.**

 MEMORY TIP

An easy way to help you remember prepositions is to think of a house. Then put as many prepositional words as you can in front of the word *house*:

above the house	*between* the house	*on* the house
around the house	*of* the house	*from* the house
behind the house	*off* the house	*with* the house
by the house	*under* the house	*to* the house
near the house	*over* the house	

The correct preposition is often determined by common practice instead of actual meaning. Learn this list of common expressions that use prepositions:

full of	interested in	call off
scared of	angry about	count on
tired of	excited about	fill in
aware of	happy about	go over
proud of	pick up	grow up
afraid of	sorry for	look up
confused by	responsible for	

APPENDIX C SKILLS REVIEW: ESL Concerns

In the following sentences, find and correct any problems with nouns, articles, verbs, and prepositions. Rewrite each sentence.

1. Few people believing that a dogs are bad for health.

_____

_____

2. Teacher in cafeteria hearded the students talking of class.

_____

_____

3. Cat running down street.

_____

_____

4. New training program be good for employees in company.

_____

_____

5. I afraid by shark in ocean.

_____

_____

6. Had you did homework for today?

_____

_____

7. I am want to keep getting good grades in math.

_____

_____

8. Most people wanting to please other people so feel accepted.

_____

_____

9. My grandfather always said, "Apple a day keeping the doctor away."

_____

_____

10. John hiding from behind the house.

_____

_____

_____

Index